Shared Joy Is Double Joy

by

Joyce Simmons

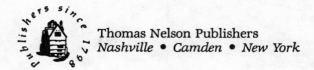

Thomas Nelson Publishers
Nashville • Camden • New York

Published in Nashville, Tennessee, by Thomas Nelson, Inc. and distributed in Canada by Lawson Falle, Ltd., Cambridge, Ontario.

Printed in the United States of America.

Scripture quotations noted NKJV are from THE NEW KING JAMES VERSION. Copyright © 1979, 1980, 1982, Thomas Nelson, Inc., Publishers.

The Bible verses marked TLB are taken from *The Living Bible* (Wheaton, Illinois: Tyndale House Publishers, 1971) and are used by permission.

The quotations on pages 100, 101, and 102 are from *How to Support Your Pastor*, copyright © 1980 by David Mains. Published by David C. Cook Publishing Co., Elgin, IL 60120. Used by permission.

Library of Congress Cataloging in Publication Data

Simmons, Joyce.
    Shared joy is double joy.

    1. Encouragement. 2. Simmons, Joyce. I. Title.
BJ1475.5.S55 1985   248.4   84-25558
ISBN 0-8407-5926-6

To my husband, Bill, my greatest encourager,
who stands behind me to urge me on, beside me to offer
  support,
and in front of me to shelter me from life's blows—
  I love you.

To my parents—Bob, Murray, Shirley, and Kelly—within
  whom the tie of encouragement was love.

To C.P. and Darleen who listened patiently to every new
  idea concerning encouragement.

Contents

Encourage Me

I wait for the silent phone to ring,
Compassionate words to bring.
My lonely heart needs to sing!
Is there no one to encourage me?

Lord, I know you're standing near.
Yet I need just one more ear,
To end the doubt and free the fear.
Is there anyone to encourage me?

I hear the knock on my door.
I know what you have sent them for.
A moment shared, I'll ask no more.
You found someone to encourage me.

Chapter 1

Encouraging
Yourself

The front door closed. I watched my husband load our car with the acoustical guitars and recorders he used in his music ministry. For the last ten years he and I had traveled together, our three boys and all our belongings stuffed into a Greyhound bus, as we drove from town to town singing in high-school gymnasiums and halls.

But tonight was different. From now on, the boys and I would be living in a small country home we had bought in Sisseton, South Dakota, so the boys could attend public school and enjoy the stability of a somewhat normal home life. Bill would still tour the Midwest as a part of the band that played with the Lowell Lundstrom evangelistic ministry, but his new schedule would permit half of his time to be spent at home with his family.

We both felt confident that the Lord had led us to this decision, one we had put off by enrolling Jason, our oldest boy, in correspondence courses for two years when he reached school age. Now that Shayne was ready for school, too, we knew both boys would benefit from attending public school and meeting others their own age.

But as I watched Bill ease out of the driveway into the street, I felt alone and empty. I was so accustomed to being a part of his ministry. Could housekeeping, caring for children, and maintaining a home by myself for part of every month fill that gap?

Our two older boys soon adjusted to the routine schedule of school and neighborhood play. The baby, chubby little Landon, and I were alone much of the day. To fill the endless hours I planned elaborate menus, devised family devotional programs, and became obsessed with protecting my tidy house from the baby's inquisitive hands. But the harder I worked to keep the house spotlessly clean, the more mischievous Landon became, uprooting plants, emptying drawers, and coloring on my newly papered wall.

One morning I suddenly became aware of a long, uninterrupted silence, which usually signaled trouble. I found Landon sitting in the bathroom in a puddle of my favorite hand lotion. His moon-sized blue eyes gazed up at mine. "See, Mom, nice hair. We go coffee?" The tub behind him was painted with my favorite Mulberry Mauve lipstick. A roll of partially unwound toilet paper spilled out from underneath the toilet seat.

"I have no time for this nonsense, young man," I scolded as I pulled his damp clothes over his sticky head and dumped him into the tub.

I became increasingly more irritable, berating my children for not appreciating my valiant efforts to become "mother and housekeeper of the year." My children didn't even realize that dust occasionally accumulated on the furniture.

One Saturday morning I insisted that the older boys clean their rooms and straighten their disheveled bookshelves. After many excuses and grumblings, they finally straggled off to the task. Minutes later Jason came out of his room, cloth in hand, face white and eyes filled with uncertainty.

"Mom," he said thoughtfully, "remember how we talked about how God created us out of dust?"

"Yes," I answered, a little puzzled.

"And isn't it true that when we die we return to dust again?" he continued.

I nodded yes.

He slumped down into a chair and covered his head with his hands. "I knew it!" he groaned. "Somebody died on top of my bookcase!"

After months of playing the perfect housewife, the strain and tension began to translate into fatigue, abdominal pain, and headaches. I had always been a very healthy person, almost critical of people who could not pull themselves up by their own bootstraps and get on with life. I reminded myself of this over and over again, but the headaches forced me to retreat to my room for hours at a time. My menstrual cycles became irregular, skipping a month or two and then returning with such pain that I soaked in a hot tub for most of an evening.

Why is this happening to me? I asked God again and again. Was he punishing me for keeping the boys at home and dividing our family?

Finally during one of my numerous trips to the doctor, he detected abdominal lumps, which seemed to appear and then disappear. "I've never seen anything like it before, Mrs. Simmons....I suggest you see a specialist."

Now I knew why God had called us to return to Sisseton. I'd come home to die!

But that wasn't the diagnosis of the specialist at the Fargo Clinic in North Dakota. Instead of the hours of examination and tests I had anticipated, the visit lasted only four or five minutes. After the doctor completed an internal examination, he patted me on the back and said, "There's nothing wrong that I can see. Go home and rest. You'll be fine." He left the examining room before I could protest.

Those words seemed harder to accept than if he had said: "You have one year to live, Mrs. Simmons." Obviously he felt that I was imagining my illness. My persistent abdominal pains and headaches must be a product of self-pity—or worse yet, a mind that was slowly losing touch with reality.

In desperation I began to cry out to God. *I always thought you were looking out for me. Have I been fooling myself, thinking I was your child?—that you really cared what happened to me? Is the sky filled with a vast loneliness rather than a Great Comforter?*

One morning about a week later I sat at the

kitchen table, sipping a cup of coffee which had become lukewarm as the minutes stretched on. It was only nine o'clock, and my housework and errands were already completed. How was I going to fill the rest of this seemingly endless day?

I picked up a copy of *Today's Christian Woman* and began to randomly flip through the pages. My eyes were caught by a series of verses at the bottom of a page:

> What a wonderful God we have—he is the Father of our Lord Jesus Christ, the source of every mercy, and the one who so wonderfully comforts and strengthens us in our hardships and trials. And why does he do this? So that when others are troubled, needing our sympathy and encouragement, we can pass on to them this same help and comfort God has given us. You can be sure that the more we undergo sufferings for Christ, the more he will shower us with his comfort and encouragement (2 Cor. 1:3-5, TLB).

I read the verses again slowly, absorbing their meaning like a dry sponge soaks up water. God seemed to be speaking to me, saying, *I need you to work for me. I know you've gone through some trials, but now you have a greater appreciation for others who are lonely, depressed, or sick. I love you and was with you all that time. Now I need you to encourage others. Can you do that for me?*

I answered, *Yes, Lord*, with the same feeling as if I had been shouting out loud. The answer came from the depths of my soul and from a newly acquired trust in God. In his wisdom, the Lord had revealed to me a ministry that could function from my home. I knew I could encourage others by a simple phone call, a note or letter, and even a quick visit.

As I studied Paul's life, I finally realized that my goals were not in the proper order. God had a broader vision for my life than I did. He wanted me to be a loving encourager to everyone, including my husband and sons. I rose each day excited about the new ministry God was suggesting.

The headaches, abdominal pain, and lethargy began to disappear as I felt God's great love healing me from within. But I knew that my own self-image was still weak, and at times I felt incapable of encouraging others.

During the past six months at home I had slid down the destructive path of self-pity, and neglected my appearance along the way. This became all too apparent to me one chilly November morning in 1982 when I tried to push my size-fourteen hips into my old size-ten slacks. The zipper creaked and finally broke under the pressure.

Just at that moment, Bill walked into the bedroom.

"Can't you see I'm getting dressed!" I snapped, humiliated that he should witness this obvious sign of a flabby body, which had expanded during my third pregnancy.

As Bill backed out the door, I heard him mutter, "You should have put the 'Beware of Woman' sign on the door!"

Tears came to my eyes as I remembered the first time my husband had deposited Landon on his brother Shayne's lap. Shayne had innocently peered up at me and asked, "Where did you get this baby, Mom? It looks like ours is still in your tummy."

I walked over and stood in front of the full-length mirror on our bedroom wall. Yes, Shayne was right. The image I saw in the mirror resembled the squat, fat reflection I used to see in the distorted mirrors at the circus. How could Bill and the kids love me when I looked like this?

For days I was lost in self-pity. As usual, I expressed my anger to the Lord. *How could you ever use anyone like me, Lord?*

I heard God answer through my thoughts: *Well, I'll admit it isn't easy for you to encourage others when you reject any compliment others give you. Don't you think I look on some things as more important than a* Glamour *magazine figure?*

Yes, I thought.

After all, when God first created man He said, "Let Us make man in Our image, according to Our Likeness" (Gen. 1:26 NKJV). David even says in the Psalms that God created us, "a little lower than the angels" and crowned us with "glory and honor" (8:5 NKJV). If God thought that much of us, who was I to belittle the particular figure that was mine? I remembered Ethel Waters's favorite line: "God don't make no flops!"

I realized that I needed something more than just believing in God, I also needed to believe his promises! In the next days, I searched through the Bible for verses to build my self-image and abolish my low opinion of myself.

I began by acknowledging that I was a child of

God. There is no apology for the human form in Psalm 139; instead David declared, "I will praise You, for I am fearfully and wonderfully made" (v. 14 NKJV).

The Bible told me that God is superior and far greater than any inferiority I felt. His people throughout the ages had proven that. Moses thought himself a poor communicator; yet, with God's help, he convinced Pharaoh to release the Israelites from their bondage in Egypt. All of the Old Testament patriarchs acknowledged God's help and guidance in their lives. In the New Testament, Paul could say, despite beatings and imprisonment, "I can do all things through Christ who strengthens me" (Phil. 4:13 NKJV).

When I read through 1 Corinthians, I heard the Lord say, "Let love be your greatest aim" (14:1 TLB) because "Love never fails" (13:8 NKJV). If God has said I can't fail, who was I to say he is wrong?

Slowly I realized that Satan was using my feelings of inferiority and inadequacy to defeat me so that I would never reach my potential as a child of God! Paul's attitude was different from mine. He confessed his imperfection—"I don't mean to say I am perfect"—but he immediately thereafter voiced his desire to "keep working toward that day when I will finally be all that Christ saved me for and wants me to be" (Phil. 3:12 TLB). He did not allow feelings of inferiority to block out his goal.

With these insights from Scripture, I glanced at myself again in the mirror. Yes, physical changes were in order. I began at the top and phoned for an appointment for a cut and perm. I set up a weight-loss program and vowed to adhere to it without losing my disposition. Finally I hung an exercise chart, which had to be filled in daily, on my bedroom door. That evening I began my first exercises—three sit-ups!

When I began to doubt my ability to maintain the discipline of my diet and exercise program, I turned to 2 Timothy: "For God has not given us a spirit of fear, but of power and of love and of a sound mind" (1:7 NKJV). God's power, not my own, would see me through.

I lost ten pounds within the first couple of weeks. After that, I was lucky to lose a pound a week. As the drudgery of trying to lose the next ten pounds began to seem overwhelming, I again turned to the Bible, where I read: "Spend your time and energy in the exercise of keeping spiritually fit. Bodily exercise is all right, but spiritual exercise is much more important and is a tonic for all you do" (1 Tim. 4:7-8 TLB).

That verse caused me to add a program of spiritual enrichment to my program of physical fitness. I began to read the stories of people like Joyce Landorf and Joni Eareckson Tada, who have led victorious lives and reached goals they had set for themselves. I listened to inspirational tapes and music as I cleaned the house and as I relaxed in the evening. I read the Bible and prayed during Landon's afternoon nap—a miraculous change since my favorite soap opera was on at this time. But, as I kept reminding myself, most of the traumas on that show were actually taking place in my own neighborhood. Why should I depress myself by viewing them again on television? Each time I was tempted to sneak a peek, I thought of two or three people whom I could help that day through a letter or phone call of encouragement.

When I began to doubt my ability to communicate God's Word because I lacked theological training, the Lord reminded me that he used the humble fishermen Peter and John as mightily as he used the intellectual Saul of Tarsus, who became Paul.

Two other areas of my life also needed discipline: my use of time and my tendency to criticize others. I began to make lists to organize my housework so I could accomplish more and be free from the nagging guilt of too many things left undone. I learned to check myself before nagging at my husband and children. *Remember, you are far from perfect*, I told myself, *so why are you expecting them to be?* After all, the scattered newspapers, dirty milk glasses, and miscellaneous shoes could be picked up in the first few minutes after the boys had gone to bed.

Soon I began to see results. Ralph Waldo Emerson once said, "A man is what he thinks about all day long." When I had spent the day feeling sorry for myself, I was impatient and irritable with my husband and children. After I began practicing spiritual discipline, I could encourage them to be themselves and assure them of my love. And miracle of all miracles, I was beginning to like the person I was becoming!

I was beginning to build a spiritual foundation, on the basis of daily Bible reading and prayer. If I hadn't been willing to examine each area of my life, I could never have begun the ministry of encouraging myself. And without the strength of this inner encouragement I never could have reached out to encourage others. I would have failed at the first sign of fatigue, given up at the slightest rejection, or doubted my faith during the personal struggles that are a part of everyday life. After all, love cannot flow from an empty cup!

An encouragement ministry is as easy to understand as the word encourage is to define. To *encourage* is "to inspire with courage, spirit, or hope." My own definition would add some other verbs to Webster's: to cheer, refresh, console, befriend, reassure, and strengthen others.

In the life and writings of the apostle Paul, I found the meaning of the ministry of encouragement. Throughout his letters to the early churches—Romans, 1 and 2 Corinthians, Galatians, Ephesians, Philippians, Colossians, Thessalonians, and 1 and 2 Timothy—he urges his readers to find the pure brotherly love that is a sign of God's people.

Paul describes the strength of this love in the second chapter of 1 Thessalonians and suggests that Christians follow the pattern that he showed them. He reminds the Thessalonians that he and Silas and Timothy had loved them "so dearly that we gave you not only God's message, but our own lives too" (1 Thess. 2:8 TLB).

An encourager or a disciple of Christ, he says, should be:

understanding and gentle—"as gentle...as a mother feeding and caring for her own children" (v. 7 TLB).

persistent and hard working—"Don't you remember, dear brothers, how hard we worked among you? Night and day we toiled and sweated to earn enough to live on so that our expenses would not be a burden to anyone there, as we preached God's Good News among you" (v. 9 TLB).

honest and pure—"pure and honest and faultless toward every one of you" (v. 10 TLB).

mature in the faith—"We talked to you as a father to his children...pleading with you, encouraging you" (v. 11 TLB).

In these verses Paul seems to be warning Christians to stay away from others who spend their days in laziness and do not follow the example he, Silas, and Timothy have set. "For you well know," he might have said, "that you ought to follow our example. You never saw us loafing. Don't waste your time with gossip. Kindly warn a brother in trouble."

God was strengthening me from within and providing a strong pillar of love to support me. Now I could feel his power. I was ready to begin to encourage other people, helping them to feel the love I felt!

The Art of Learning to Love Yourself by Cecil Osborne (Zondervan Publishing House)

You Can Pray with Power by Lowell Lundstrom (Lundstrom Ministries)

Three Steps Forward, Two Steps Back by Charles R. Swindoll (Thomas Nelson Publishers)

How to Get Up When You're Down by Lowell Lundstrom (Lundstrom Ministries)

Not I, But Christ by Corrie ten Boom (Thomas Nelson Publishers)

Notes

Chapter 2

Encouraging
Your Mate

I met my husband, Bill, on September 18, 1972. I had just finished a two-week stretch of duty as a nurse at the Winnipeg General Hospital in Canada. Finally, I had a free evening to relax; and at first I rejected my sister's invitation to go to a young adult rally at church. Then I gave in and went along to please her. I did not realize the future importance of that seemingly inconsequential decision.

When we arrived in the sanctuary, a family musical group, the Simmons Singers, was busy setting up their amplifiers, acoustical guitars, and drums on the crowded, little platform.

Oh, great! I thought. *An evening of loud guitar music—just what I needed!* The only music I could imagine enjoying that evening would have been from my favorite mellow album, *Praise Strings.*

Soon a curly haired young man, carrying a contraption that reminded me of an ironing board, equipped with pedals on the bottom and strings on top, stumbled up the stairs to join the others. He sat down, strapped the instrument around himself, and placed steel picks on each finger. The combination of his novel instrument and his good looks held my attention as the program began.

I was surprised when Rick Simmons, the head of the group, introduced this young man as his son, Bill, a steel guitar player. Rick and his wife, Lil, looked too young to be the parents of this young man and of Darleen, Bill's sister, who played the bass and sang. Several times I felt as if Bill Simmons was looking at me, even smiling in my direction; but I rationalized that it was merely good eye contact, an entertainer's way of involving the audience.

After the service, I learned differently. My sister Shirley wanted to accept the Simmonses' invitation to meet them. She introduced herself to Lil, and their conversation soon became quite animated.

"I really must tell you," Lil finally said, "we were amazed when you and your sister came in. She looks so much like our son's past girlfriend. We've teased him about it all evening!"

Without hesitation, my sister went across the church to Bill Simmons, grabbed his hand, and brought him over. I'm sure she thought she had finally found a man for her sister!

Bill took it all in stride, admitting that I did indeed look like his former girlfriend. Then he asked if I would go out for coffee with him. Of course, I agreed. We were so at ease with each other that we talked until early the next morning.

A few months later I left to attend a small Bible college in Eston, Saskatchewan. Whenever Bill and his family were close to the area, he came to visit me. Between visits he sent crazy letters and parcels. One day I opened an envelope to the unrelenting stare of a plastic eyeball. The note accompanying it said, "I'm keeping an eye on you." I had been immediately attracted to his good looks, and I was growing to love his outgoing personality.

On New Year's Eve of 1972, Bill proposed to me. Four months later we were married in that same small church where we had met. We had only a three-day honeymoon before we joined his family in their full-time ministry of evangelism, and moved into their new motor home, where the entire family slept and traveled. There were no moments to be alone, no time to adjust to each other. We were either traveling from town to town with Bill's family or staying in the homes of members of the churches we visited. Often our hosts kept us up late into the evening and early morning, asking questions about our ministry. "It must be so exciting to travel all over the country," they would say, again and again. "Tell us where you've been." Finally, they would exclaim wistfully, "How lucky you are to travel all together as one big, happy family!"

Three months after we were married I became pregnant, and my energy level often waned. Bill remained active, anxious to be busy, so the few times we could have been alone together, he was usually off to some music store or pawn shop to find a "great" buy. I became withdrawn and sullen when he left me alone.

Each week we seemed to discover something new and not necessarily attractive about each other. I no longer laughed at all his jokes. To my surprise, he had a red-hot, combustible temper, which made me run for cover when it erupted. The good attributes we had first seen in each other remained, but our attitudes toward them began to change.

About the time our first son, Jason, was born, Bill's family decided to give up their traveling ministry, and his father regained his position as a journeyman welder at a large steel factory in Winnipeg. I was excited about the change; now Bill and I and our little son would be a normal family. We could pop popcorn together in the evenings, sit around the fireplace in our own home, and talk about silly little things as we had done during our courtship.

But Bill was not ready to settle into what he saw as a humdrum existence. He was a talented guitar player and singer who wanted to use his ability for God. When Jason was only two days old, Lowell Lundstrom of Sisseton, South Dakota, phoned to ask Bill to play guitar with his group. Bill was ecstatic! Five days later, with a week-old baby, we drove the 350 miles to Sisseton as Bill cheerily described the wonderful life ahead.

When we arrived, Lowell's two daughters, Londa and Lisa, immediately adopted Jason, while Connie, his wife, showed us through the forty-foot bus which stood in front of the ministry's office. We stepped out of the bright summer sunshine to enter the dark, cavelike interior of the bus. Both sides were lined with bunks and an occasional closet for the fourteen people who traveled with the ministry. A small, built-in bathroom in the rear was very obviously in need of a plumber.

Bill and I were to share a bottom bunk, three and a half feet by five feet, eight inches, in the front section. A space on the top bunk would be partially cleared of the musical instruments and amplifiers for Jason.

As we pushed our things into the one small drawer we would call our own, Bill exclaimed, "This is going to be great!"

I silently grumbled, *O Lord, please deliver me!* My fears were proven true. Our small baby had to sleep, rather unsuccessfully, despite the noise of the stereo system's music, which blared long into the night to keep the driver awake as he drove to the next town. I felt that I had to keep Jason quiet when he cried during the night, so I was constantly getting up to rock or feed him. Though I knew it sometimes was beneficial, there was no way this baby could be left "to cry it out" for one night as is sometimes necessary to properly adjust his feeding and sleeping schedule.

If it hadn't been for the Lundstroms' genuine love and the worthwhile goal of their ministry, I could never have endured the next seven years, with the rigorous schedule of three hundred rallies a year. Each day our group traveled another bumpy road to a new church, set up the instru-

ments and necessary gear, performed and wit-
nessed, tore down the equipment, and loaded it
onto the bus so we could travel all night to make
our next performance.

While the team performed, I sat on the bus with
our growing family, which now consisted of two
little boys. Jason and Shayne often found it difficult
to be restrained in such small quarters. I wanted
my husband to break loose from the group so we
could go home to our families in Winnipeg.

I tried to smother my discontent so Bill and I
could keep up the front of "a perfect young Chris-
tian couple," but my disappointment slowly grew
into bitterness and despair. Prince Charming
hadn't whisked me away to a life of bliss, as I had
always dreamed. Most of the time Bill was too tired
from crusades to notice me or my needs. I was sure
he thought of me as a complaining and ungrateful
wife who didn't appreciate what she had. Now I
think there may have been some truth in that, but
then I believed myself to resemble the sweet, com-
pliant Cinderella more than the wicked step-
mother.

Bill and I avoided talking about our problems, be-
cause we didn't understand them or know how to
solve them. In our own ways we still cared for each
other and loved our ministry, but the strong feel-
ings we once had felt for each other were slowly
being strangled.

After several years, I began singing with the
group, which helped me to feel more a part of the
ministry. But being on the platform, rehearsing for
hours each day, and recording put even more

strain on me and our marriage. I constantly worried that the boys, who sometimes played happily backstage while we performed, would fight or, as they had been known to do, peek out from behind the backdrop so the audience could see them.

Bill and I were never alone. The entire group lived and slept within speaking distance of one another. We even ate together around large tables at restaurants. Everyone knew when a couple was fighting or when a child was sick or when someone was depressed or disillusioned. So it was not surprising that Allen, who also sang with the group, recognized my frustration. He seemed to see the hurt and loneliness in my eyes and respond with a glance that said, "I know and I care."

Often when he and I passed each other, he touched my arm gently and said, "You really look lovely today," or gave me some other small compliment.

I began to look forward to these short encounters, which revived some of the excitement I remembered from Bill's and my courtship. Maybe Allen was Prince Charming and I had been wrong to marry Bill. Thoughts like this made me feel guilty. A Christian wife should not be attracted to a man other than her husband. Would my feelings someday get out of control and overcome my Christian beliefs? This continual conflict of my emotions and my conscience sapped the little extra energy I had.

But, just as suddenly as Allen's attentions began, they stopped. He no longer gave me compliments or listened to my problems. I was confused until I saw him in a restaurant one day and overheard him giving the lovely young lady beside him the same compliments he had lavished on me.

Suddenly I realized that Allen played an emotional game with people. *Why hadn't I known better?* I wondered to myself. I felt more rejected and defeated than I had before.

Several weeks later Bill and I were eating lunch in a restaurant when, through the window, I saw a young couple walking hand-in-hand. Once they reached the car, he lovingly opened the door. Cinderella/Prince Charming love did exist. Bill and I were just among the few who had missed it! I began to cry and couldn't stop.

At first Bill tried to joke. "I didn't think the food was that bad!" Then he realized how upset I was, and he suggested we take a walk.

Under the shade of a giant oak, I began to unload the years of bitterness and resentment—every incident I could remember. Once I had clearly outlined his faults, I acknowledged my own failures as a person and a wife, ending with my emotional attachment to Allen. I felt that Bill had a right to leave me, even though I had never had a physical relationship with Allen.

Instead he held me lovingly in his arms as his tears mingled with mine. He confessed that he, too, was disappointed with our relationship, only he had buried his resentment through deeper involvement in his work and his music. He pointed out some of the ways I had let him down, not in an accusatory or judgmental way, but to share his pain and sorrow.

That day, under the giant oak, I again saw the *man* I had fallen in love with—a man who truly loved me; a man I truly loved. It was the beginning of unconditional forgiveness. Oh, we had forgiven each other in the past, but there was always a price tag on that forgiveness. "I'll love and forgive you if...I'll love and forgive you when...I'll love and forgive you, but...." Forgiveness was just another tool we used to judge and reform each other.

Now we committed ourselves to unconditional forgiveness, releasing each other from any indebtedness for past actions, and thereby allowing ourselves to be free to begin again in our own unique way, not according to a predetermined plan set down by one or the other. Such unconditional forgiveness is suggested by Paul in Colossians. Why we hadn't seen it before this I don't know, but now we tried to live by these verses:

> Since you have been chosen by God who has given you this new kind of life, and because of his deep love and concern for you, you should practice tenderhearted mercy and kindness to others....Be gentle and ready to forgive; never hold grudges. Remember, the Lord forgave you, so you must forgive others (Col. 3:12-13 TLB).

We began to notice that other couples played the same game of "one upmanship" we had played. They seemed to derive satisfaction from each other's discomfort at making a mistake and in taking revenge. Phony forgiveness, Bill and I now realized, just adds to the destruction of a relationship rather than its healing. Jesus showed us what true forgiveness is when he said from the cross, "Father, forgive them; for they do not know what they do" (Luke 23:34 NKJV).

Neither my husband nor I had fully understood how we were hurting one another; instead, with our self-centered tunnel vision, we had seen only how we were being offended. Once we began to share our hurts more openly, each of us was better able to see our marriage from the other's point of view. We could begin to say with Jesus, "Father, forgive [him/her] for [he/she] doesn't know what [he/she] is doing."

We also vowed to commit ourselves to a new type of relationship, one that was closer to Paul's admonition: "Stop being mean, bad-tempered and angry. Quarreling, harsh words, and dislike of others should have no place in your lives" (Eph. 4:31 TLB).

I'm not saying that we became perfect marriage partners. We cannot expect perfection in this world, either from ourselves or others. After all, we live in a world that became fallen and imperfect when Adam and Eve bit into the forbidden fruit in the Garden of Eden.

That couple walking hand-in-hand to the car outside that restaurant seemed perfectly in love at that moment. But I wasn't around to see them when they were fighting over finances or some other problem.

God calls us to forgive each other's imperfections, for He reminds us: "Your heavenly Father will forgive you if you forgive those who sin against you; but if *you* refuse to forgive *them*, *he* will not forgive *you*" (Matt. 6:14-15 TLB).

Some people might ask, "Don't you feel awful

that you wasted eight years of your marriage?"

No, I praise God every day that it took us no more than eight years to realize that true love is based on unconditional forgiveness. Now Bill and I look forward to the future, based on the relationship we have, not as it was or would be if....Our Prince Charming/Cinderella fantasies have been replaced by the reality of the work that is required to make a marriage run smoothly.

Sometimes a quiet dinner for two at a restaurant helps us communicate our feelings more clearly than we could at home with the boys interrupting us. Other times we stop our car by the side of a secluded road and discuss our problems positively, rather than attacking each other's faults. We often work together around the house and have found that doing the dishes can be an opportunity to visit with one another.

Bill still travels frequently. When he is packing and his suitcase is open on the bed, I slip notes inside his socks or clothing—or I write "I love you" on his notebook. These intimate messages encourage him when he is away from home. Sometimes he'll call during the middle of the day just to tell me he loves me or is thinking of me. Other times he sends flowers or cards with his original verses.

Bill calls me "Pretty Girl" when I'm in my flannel nightie with rollers in my hair and old slippers on my feet, as well as when I'm wearing a pretty new dress and shoes. He's learned that some days I'm totally irrational, and he sits through my crab sessions, no matter how trivial the problem seems.

These opportunities to vent my frustrations help erode the tension that used to build between us until it reached the inevitable explosions.

Bill and I have learned to live with each other's faults and weaknesses—and even laugh about them! One day Bill looked at me and said, "You know, I'm keeping a record of all the good times we've had together."

Excitedly I replied, "Oh, are you keeping a diary?"

"No," he laughed, "the stubs of my checkbook."

We have learned not to depend entirely on each other for happiness, since we are human and can fail each other unintentionally. Instead of expecting each other to be perfect, we look to the one true God for perfection and joy. We have placed our faith in something stronger and more stable than any marriage could ever be: the love of a forgiving Heavenly Father. It is not possible for us to have devotions together on a daily basis, but each of us has learned how important it is to be filled with the Word of God.

Roberta Flack, the singer, once said on a TV talk show, "Getting married is easy; staying married is more difficult; staying happily married for a lifetime should rank among the finest arts."

Bill and I have discovered that with God's love, marriage can survive. It can even be the joyous union God intended it to be!

Try writing a few of the following notes to encourage your husband. Then begin to create your own, which will be even more meaningful. If you keep praying not only for your mate, but also for yourself, the change may be contagious!

We may not have a hundred years,
Our days on earth may be few.
But I'm glad for this one moment
To share my love with you.

I wish I had listened
A little more closely today.
I knew you needed someone
To share what you had to say.

I get a little too busy
With things that never get done.
But I'm learning to see more important things—
Be patient with me, hon!

We may have different opinions.
We may not always agree.
But one thing is never in question:
You were meant for me.

Promise me we'll always grow
Closer every day.
When things are tough and they go wrong,
We'll always find a way.

Leave a note suggesting a secret meeting. Here's one I left for Bill:

Meet you at Country Kitchen,
About a quarter to four.
I'll be the brunette waiting for you
Beside the big front door.

The Christian Couple by Larry Christenson (Bethany Fellowship Publishers)

Maximum Marriage by Tim Timmons (Revell)

Heaven's Answer for the Home by Lowell Lundstrom (Lundstrom Ministries)

How to Be Happy though Married by Tim LaHaye (Tyndale)

101 Ways to Your Husband's/Wife's Heart by Nick and Rosie Allan (Thomas Nelson Publishers)

Notes

Chapter 3

Encouraging
Your Children

The sound of three cuckoos from our cuckoo clock every afternoon used to be like the old-fashioned bugle sounding the call to battle. The two oldest boys, Jason and Shayne, would burst in the door, releasing all the energy that had been contained during a long school day. Books, coats, tote bags, everything would be thrown in the closest chair or corner. Neither boy could wait to tell of his newest triumph—a good grade on a recent test—or sorrow—the unmerciful way some classmate had teased him—so they always tried to outshout each other to gain my attention.

I'm sure this scene occurs in other homes in the United States. For my part I had my own set of special greetings for the children: "Get those muddy shoes off immediately! You're tracking mud all over the carpet." Or "Hey, don't drop those books there. Take them to your room. I've spent all day cleaning." And "Don't leave the milk out after you have your snack. How many times do I have to say the same thing!" Soon everyone was yelling—and no one was listening!

Sometimes my boys have rebelled at my harsh words, like the day they put their coats on and went back outside. Moments later our next-door neighbor called to ask, "Is it all right if the boys have milk and cookies with our girls and then spend the afternoon?"

Finally I realized that I was so busy trying to be a perfect housekeeper (though no one else noticed or cared that the house was clean) that I wasn't giving the boys the love and understanding they needed. Often I was expecting them to act like miniature adults, rather than children.

We had begun to evaluate our roles as parents two years earlier when we had finally decided to settle in Sisseton. Early in 1981 I read the book *Be All You Can Be* by David Augsburger. His description of the "prodigal parent" fit too closely the life style Bill and I had developed:

Keep your schedule too full with outside-the-home activities to spend time playing, and just being with your kids. Keep your mind too full with outside plans and ideas to give time listening to them. Keep your heart too full of outside-the-home loyalties and responsibilities to have time for loving them. Keep your relationship simple; don't get too involved, that takes time and energy, understanding, insight, that should be going into your business or profession. Don't try and understand them, you probably wouldn't anyway. Why waste the effort? Don't get involved in discipline. Keep on their good side, give them what they want.[1]

As Bill and I considered each sentence, we realized that we were, according to Augsburger's criteria, almost perfect "prodigal parents." Why were we neglecting the children we adored? We knew the answer: Our strenuous travel schedule had caused us to try to mold their childhood into adult life styles. And our exhaustion from this schedule kept us from using the little time that was available for family activities. The decision was inevitable: The boys had to be given a more "normal" home life.

But I quickly discovered that a parent's job is almost as frustrating in a "settled" home as it is in a bus, especially since I was alone with the boys much of the time. Our oldest son, Jason, is very outgoing and full of energy, just like his dad. Bill and I had worked hard to contain his aggressive and determined personality. Now I had to say "No!" to him by myself—and stick to my decision despite the four thousand reasons he gave to make me change my mind!

I reminded myself of what Henry Ward Beecher, a preacher many years ago, once said: "The energy which makes a child hard to manage is the energy which afterwards makes him the manager of life." I didn't want to squelch Jason's potential, but I knew I had to help him learn to control his impulsiveness—and I had to do it lovingly, without showing the strong anger and resentment I sometimes felt. Soon I realized that I had to have the same unconditional love for my children I had learned to have for my husband.

Only God's power could help me control my anger when Jason or Shayne trailed across my new carpet with muddy boots. I repeated the apostle Paul's words in my mind: "I can do all things through Christ who strengthens me" (Phil. 4:13 NKJV).

I have learned that children require *agape* love, from the Greek word meaning an unselfish, sacrificial love. George Sweeting in his book, *Catch the Spirit of Love*, reminds us that this love springs "from a sense of the preciousness of the object loved. It is a love of esteem, of valuing." The word *agape*, Sweeting tells us, "is seldom found in classical Greek; the pagan world apparently was unaware of its reality. The source of *agape* love is God Himself."[2]

The prophet Jeremiah told the Israelites that God loves us in just this way, for the Lord appeared to him, saying: "Yes, I have loved you with an everlasting love" (Jer. 31:3 NKJV). And God's continuous forgiveness of the Hebrew nation when they disobeyed him shows this kind of love in action.

I became determined to practice *agape* love when natural love was impossible—as on the day the boys were playing in their room and felt nature's call. They opened the dresser drawer and urinated into the clean clothes. Their excuse? "We were too busy to go all the way to the washroom, Mother."

Agape love doesn't ask me to smile and say, "That's OK. Do it anytime." But it does require that my punishment be fair and made without unreasonable anger. Having the boys carry the clothes to the washer and help me wash and dry them seemed a good way to help them remember certain rules of conduct.

At times like this I have also reminded myself of the many occasions I have gone before the Lord to confess my sins and shortcomings. If His reaction had been, "Get out of here. How could you do such a thing?", I would have been crushed. Instead the Lord listened and then forgave me. He asks me, in turn, to treat my children with the same love and forgiveness.

I never enjoy disciplining my children, but I consider fair discipline to be a form of encouragement, the kind that encourages children to think twice before making the same mistake.

One day I overhead Jason and Shayne arguing with each other. "You tell her, Shayne," Jason said.

"I'm not going to tell her. *You* tell her," Shayne replied.

"If you tell her," said Jason, "she won't spank us."

"You go tell her," Shayne insisted. "You've known her longer than I have!"

The boys had been playing with a football in the living room, a real no-no, and had broken a pink Chinese vase. I took the ball away from them for a week, which I knew was greater punishment than a spanking.

But a few days later, I discovered that the ball wasn't where I had put it. The boys figured Mom had forgotten the incident and had retrieved the ball and tucked it neatly under their bed. This time they were spanked soundly for their disobedience: They had not learned their lesson the first time.

The parents' role is an extension of God's relationship with us, and the apostle Paul encourages Christians to allow God to train and correct us:

> Let God train you, for he is doing what any loving father does for his children. Whoever heard of a son who was never corrected? If God doesn't punish you when you need it, as other fathers punish their sons, then it means that you aren't really God's son at all—that you don't really belong in his family....Our earthly fathers trained us for a few brief years, doing the best for us that they knew how, but God's correction is always right and for our best good, that we may share his holiness. Being punished isn't enjoyable while it is happening—it hurts! But afterwards we can see the result, a quiet growth in grace and character (Heb. 12:7-11 TLB).

The next verses are particularly meaningful to me as a parent: "So take a new grip with your tired hands, stand firm on your shaky legs, and mark out a straight, smooth path for your feet so that those who follow you, though weak and lame, will not fall and hurt themselves, but become strong" (vv. 12-13 TLB).

Sometimes I can stop my boys from doing something that is wrong with a more appropriate response than punishment. One day I noticed that Shayne was walking deliberately in front of the TV so Jason couldn't see his favorite show. Then, seeming to tire of tormenting Jason, he began to tease Landon, taking his toys away from him and purposely tripping him as he toddled across the living room floor.

I took Shayne to the kitchen and sat him on my knee, holding him tightly for a while. Finally I asked him, "What's the matter? You don't seem to be yourself today."

Reluctantly, he admitted that he missed his dad, who had been gone for nine days. After admitting, "I miss Dad, too," I suggested that we draw pictures together; when he tired of that, we read some jokes from a favorite book. Forty-five minutes later, Shayne was outside playing happily with the neighborhood children. Spanking Shayne for mistreating his brothers would only have added to his problem.

Rudolf Dreikurs, in his book *Children: The Challenge*, points out the importance of encouraging a child:

> Encouragement is more important than any other aspect of child raising. It is so important that the lack of it can be the basic cause for misbehavior. Each child needs continuous encouragement just as a plant needs water. He cannot grow, develop, or gain a sense of belonging without encouragement.[3]

My oldest son's first year in public school was quite difficult for him because he did not know how to interact with kids his own age. One night after I had disciplined him for getting into trouble at school, I found him lying on the floor in my room reading a book.

When I looked closely, I saw that the book was one of three journals I keep in my nightstand. Each one is a record of the outstanding or funny things each boy does, how much he is loved, and the special times we have together. These journals were supposed to be secret; I had planned to give them to the boys once they were grown.

Half-curious, half-angry, I asked Jason why he was reading the journal.

"I read it a lot, Mom," he confessed, "every time I feel down or get into trouble, I come in here and read this book. It tells me how much you really love me and how special I am to you and Dad. I feel good inside again, knowing I am worth so much to somebody."

By the end of my first year at home, I began to realize that I loved my new job as a homemaker. I no longer envied the career woman's expensive clothes and executive position; training my children to assume their place as God's children was the greatest career I could have! I set out to enjoy the times the children and I spent together.

Some days I would be dressed in my jeans and old jacket, waiting for them on the steps when they came home from school. I'm not much of a tackle or guard, but we could throw the football around and enjoy the exercise. Other days I would pack a lunch, and the two older boys and I would ride our bikes, with Landon stuffed into the tyke seat on my fender, to some adventurous new spot for a picnic. Sometimes I planned shopping and errands so I could pick up the kids at school and take them out for a treat.

The snowy hills behind our house are great for tobogganing! Though I often groaned and pleaded with the boys to do something else, after I was dressed in five layers of warm clothes, I enjoyed those afternoons. So did my sons, despite my high-pitched screaming as we sped down the hill!

After supper I often help Jason with his homework. His mediocre grades resemble my own, but I don't hide my academic weaknesses; it is good for him to realize Mom and Dad had to work hard in school. Other evenings Shayne and I read about stars and spaceships in one of his encyclopedias, or from one of the many other books that fill the shelves in the older boys' room.

Sometimes I leave love notes on the head of their beds or on the bathroom mirror—any place where they will see them easily. Jason once opened his lunch box in the school lunch room and found a note in big, black letters: "Mama loves you!" The other boys' reaction taught me to limit his notes to secret places.

During those times when each boy needs individual attention, I try to take him for a walk down our country road or out to a local restaurant. They tell me things during these private times that I never hear when the entire family is present. Sometimes, in order to keep their confidence, I have to hide my anger or disappointment when they tell me they have been involved in fights at school.

We turned the basement into a playroom for the boys so they could enjoy their activities and I could still keep the house organized. I also posted a chart of household chores on the refrigerator and pasted funny-faced stickers or stars beside each boy's name when a job was done correctly. The weekend yard jobs of weeding and planting and raking leaves have become family fun activities instead of chores, because we end the day with a picnic under our favorite apple tree.

Once in a while we have a special pajama party limited to family members, which makes the kids feel that being a part of the family is special. We sing songs and tell stories, munch on popcorn, stay up later than usual, and all sleep in sleeping bags or on blankets in the living room.

We have also made an effort to enrich our family devotions by acting out skits and stories and having Bible quizzes and memory-verse contests. Books we find in our local Christian bookstore give us other creative ideas, such as recipes for snacks. We have even made our own activity book, with games and puzzles the boys create themselves.

Many times we have talked through misunderstandings and fears the boys bring home from school. Jason was upset the day a high school student yelled at him, "Hey, kid, why are you carrying around that crazy bag?" Pointing to the word *Lundstroms* printed on the side, he taunted, "Are you a Christian? You better get rid of that bag!"

"Sure, I'm a Christian," Jason answered innocently. "Isn't everybody?"

The boy left without harassing him further, but poor Jason couldn't understand why the boy was picking on him in the first place. We explained that high school boys who feel inferior sometimes take out their frustrations on little kids. Jason felt better and vowed not to tease little kids when he grows up.

The importance of responding to the boys' questions or comments came through to me one day when I was visiting a friend who was having problems with depression and discouragement. My friend and I had just agreed to reject negative responses, which are often our natural reaction, for more positive, constructive ones, when her little red-haired boy tumbled in the door from school. He began to describe something that had happened at school, but his mother interrupted him with: "Don't talk to me now. I'm busy. Besides, I don't want to hear any more about that dumb teacher; she doesn't know anything anyway. Don't bug me with those notes she sends home; I've had it with all that garbage."

Later as I was pulling on my snow boots to leave, I saw this little redhead push the cat off the top of the TV. "Don't you know anything, ya dumb cat?" he yelled. "Get off the stupid TV. You shouldn't be on top of it, even though there's nothing on but yucky shows and a thousand commercials!" I suddenly realized how much influence parents' attitudes have on children.

Children listen to us far more closely than we imagine they do. In fact, they often become our mirrors, reflecting the best and the worst attitudes they have observed in their home environment.

Most of what I have said here is about young children, since that is my particular experience. However, grownup children need encouragement, too. Many parents of married children have the "gift of time," and are able to write letters of encouragement to their children, even if the kids don't always respond. I know that love letters from my own mom and dad who live twenty-five hundred miles away have lifted my spirits on lots of blue days.

Grandparents can also encourage their grandchildren with postcards and letters. Kids love to get mail. It seems to confirm their place in the family when they receive mail just like adults. And children frequently ask their grandparents, "Tell me about when you were young" or "Tell me another story about my mommy [daddy] as a little girl [boy]."

Our ancestry is an important part of our identity, and a close relationship with grandparents is a blessing to every child. Our Jason said to Bill one night as he was being tucked into bed, "You know what, Dad, I've decided to get married. And I'm going to marry Grandma!"

"You can't marry my mother," Bill laughed.

"Why not?" Jason retorted. "You married mine!"

Some days seem hard at school.
You can't do anything right.
But remember, no matter what goes on—
You're never out of God's sight.

Before you close your sleepy eyes,
Talk to God tonight.
And if you forget, remember this—
He's there in the morning light.

Sharing your feelings is hard sometimes;
You don't know what to say.
But God already knows how you feel.
Let him share your day.

Just wanted to remind you
To read God's Word.
There're stories of heroes and lions and kings,
The best you've ever heard.

Prayer is just talking to God,
Not only when things are bad.
He likes to hear when things go good.
He's happy when you're glad!

Life isn't always fair, is it?
Especially if you're a teenager.
But God understands at every age.
Remember, He's always there.

Your teenage years are special.
You're changing we can see.
But even though you're growing up,
God holds you on His knee.

The choices we make as teenagers
Matter down the road.
If you're worried about making the right ones,
Let Jesus lighten your load.

God loves you
   —not for what you should be,
   —not for what people want you to be,
   —but for what you are.
You're His.

When people tend to put you down,
And you don't know what to do,
Take your eyes from them to Him.
His love is watching you.

What Happens When Children Grow by M. Jacobsen (Victor Books)

You and Your Child by Charles Swindoll (Thomas Nelson Publishers)

Know Your Child by Joe Temple (Baker Books)

Train Up a Child by Dr. Harold J. Sala (Accent)

Suggested reading for children

God Cares When I Don't Like Myself by Elspeth Murphy (Chariot Books) or any other book in the *God's Word in My Heart* series

Special Times with God by David and Naomi Shibley (Thomas Nelson Publishers)

Look What You've Done Now, Moses by Fredrick and Patricia McKissack (Chariot Books) or any other book in the *I Love To Read* series

Droodles Ten Commandments Storybook by Ray Cioni (Chariot Books)

Listen to the Animals by Bill Coleman (Bethany Fellowship)

The Christian Kids Almanac by Robert Flood (Chariot Books)

Just for Kids Album by Lowell Lundstrom Ministries

Notes

Chapter 4

Encouraging
Your Friends

I sat in a local restaurant in the fall of 1981 listening to Norma as she revealed intimate, disturbing details about her husband, Greg, and their marriage. In my mind, I could see a similar scene when the two of us had visited several years before. At that time I had been spiritually immature and had tried to console Norma by agreeing with her. I had even asked, "Why do you stay married to him?"

Norma had suddenly become quiet and our visit soon ended. Norma hurried home to tell her husband everything I had said. Within a few hours, a red-faced, furious Greg appeared at my door, shouting, "Where'd you get your credentials, lady? Did you write a book on how to be a know-it-all? Because I'm here to tell you, you know nothing, nothing at all!"

By the time I had figured out what he was talking about he was long gone. After hearing Norma's second recounting of her problems, I felt like saying to her, "Hey, you don't think I'm going to listen to this again, do you? After all, I know the old adage, 'Fooled once, shame on you, but fooled twice, shame on me.' "

Still I sat there as Norma maliciously vowed to get even with Greg for the way he treated her. *Why did I continue to get involved with Norma—or with other friends who had let me down over the years, friends who only called when they needed a babysitter or some service done for them?* I asked myself. *And what about the other friends who criticized me behind my back? And the ones who seemed to genuinely care for me but too frequently shared my problems with others for "prayer"?*

At one time I had felt much like the famous painter, James Abbott McNeill Whistler, who was seated next to a patronizing young English lord at an aristocratic dinner party. During a lull in the conversation, the pompous young man had adjusted his monocle and leaned toward Whistler, "Ah, y'know, Mr. Whistler," he had drawled, "I passed your house this mawning."

"Thank you," Whistler had replied courteously. "Thank you for passing by."

Many times in the past I had avoided some of my so-called "friends" or encouraged them to "pass me by," so I wouldn't have to hear their problems and become involved. However, I began to feel that God was calling me to listen so I could encourage them.

I had been reading in the Bible about Barnabas, whose name meant "son of encouragement." You don't hear a whole lot about him, because he was always standing beside his famous friends—like the apostle Paul and Mark—helping them, rather than being in the spotlight himself.

But it was Barnabas who accepted the converted Saul of Tarsus when other Christians were still suspicious of him because he was a well-known persecutor of Christians. It was Barnabas who put his reputation on the line to back Paul because he believed that Paul's faith and talents would help build the young church. It was Barnabas who stepped back to accept a position as Paul's trusted companion and sidekick because he recognized Paul as the leader. The Book of Acts is full of accounts in which Barnabas helped Paul become the evangelist of the Mediterranean.

When Paul wanted to drop John Mark from the second missionary trip, Barnabas stood his ground against Paul. Barnabas saw beyond Mark's youth, which had caused him to buckle under the stress of the first missionary journey, to the potential strength of the disciple.

Barnabas and Paul parted company, but they remained friends. Barnabas took John Mark and sailed to Cyprus; Paul chose another companion, Silas, and went to Asia Minor. In parting they doubled their outreach for the Lord. Disagreements between friends can lead to greater things—if resentment and anger are absent. How many of us today enable our friends to become all they can be? Do we always see the best in persons as Barnabas did?

In his epistles, Paul tells Christians that Christ has

given us the ministry of reconciliation. "Therefore we are ambassadors for Christ, as though God were pleading through us: we implore *you* on Christ's behalf, be reconciled to God" (2 Cor. 5:20 NKJV).

Certainly it was God's love and his written Word that changed my life. I knew that three steps had been important to my spiritual growth: (1) studying God's Word, (2) relying on God's strength and direction through the guidance of prayer, and (3) giving over my life to the leading of the Holy Spirit, so I could truly say what Jesus said in the Garden of Gethsemane: "Not my will, but Yours, be done" (Luke 22:42 NKJV). Now I wanted to help my friends follow these steps to find the same peace.

Encouraging and loving our friends is sometimes the supreme test, but Jesus asks us to keep trying to "love each other just as much as I love you" (John 13:34 TLB). Why? Because "Your strong love for each other will prove to the world that you are my disciples" (John 13:35 TLB).

I once heard it said that "Silence is golden, except when it comes to witnessing; then it's plain yellow." Witnessing is hard for many of us, especially when it comes to saying the direct words, "Do you know Christ as your personal Lord and Savior?" But witnessing to our friends sometimes involves much more than preaching to them. It involves a commitment of time—months and years of being compassionate, loving, and understanding when our friends have problems.

I sat in the restaurant that day in 1981 listening to Norma with a compassionate, loving attitude. I sensed that her problem was not really her husband, but her constant rejection of him and her determination to have her own way. She blamed Greg for not always taking her side in arguments with the kids, yet in front of the children she criticized his ability to lead their family. She harped at him for not conducting family devotions, but she could never find the time to become involved in church activities herself.

Norma always had a sarcastic response to any compliment Greg tried to give her. On the night of their fifteenth anniversary, we had joined them for a celebration supper. Greg tried to begin the evening positively by saying to Norma, "Honey, I can't believe we've been married for fifteen years. You look just the same to me."

Without hesitation, Norma replied, "I should. I'm wearing the same dress!"

I know I must accept my friends just as Christ has accepted me. If I don't, I am judging them, and Scripture warns us: "Judge not, that you be not judged. For with what judgment you judge, you will be judged; and with the same measure you use, it will be measured back to you" (Matt. 7:1-2 NKJV). I am counting on Christ's forgiveness to eliminate my own sins; I certainly do not want him to judge me by the critical standards of this world.

Such judgment and criticism only breed bitterness and hard feelings. As Norman Vincent Peale once said, "Most of us would rather be revived by praise than saved by criticism."

After I overcame my own selfishness, I was able to tell Norma how the Lord could help her. "If you just commit yourself to him and reach out to him through daily Bible study and prayer, I know he will help you." How different this counsel was from the last advice I had given her!

It is easy to sit and sympathize with a friend, but to really see their need requires the power of the Holy Spirit. In this conversation with Norma, the Holy Spirit reminded me of my past failures and showed me the particular part of my experience Norma needed to hear.

The Holy Spirit also helped me to understand the guidance Scripture gives us and to apply it to Norma's situation. Once I showed her that we are mirrors, reflecting God's image to our families, she began to understand the importance of becoming "more like him."

The apostle Paul encourages us to do this: "But we Christians have no veil over our faces; we can be mirrors that brightly reflect the glory of the Lord. And as the Spirit of the Lord works within us, we become more and more like him" (2 Cor. 3:18 TLB).

Finally I could count on the Holy Spirit to help Norma see the wisdom of what I had shared. Once she realized that she was directly responsible to God for her own behavior, she began to review and inspect her own critical nature. Greg was soon impressed with the change in his wife.

When I am having trouble loving a friend like Norma, I follow three steps:

   1. Clear up any obvious problems by taking the initiative to admit my failure in the relationship and ask for forgiveness.

2. Find some common interest and begin a new friendship there.
3. Raise the person up to the Lord in prayer.

As you have seen in my experience, you must be growing spiritually before you can minister to others. I'm sure my earlier meddling did Norma and Greg more harm than good. Because my encouragement is now based on biblical truth, which is a part of my life, it is a blessing to my friends.

I clipped a guide out of *Be All You Can Be* by David Augsburger so I could assess my ministry of encouragement. If I feel I'm slipping, I read through these suggestions:

If you trust someone
1. You believe the best of a friend until it is proven otherwise.
2. You wish the best for an enemy, though he deserves otherwise.
3. You silence all gossip about the author until the truth can be seen as true.
4. You refuse to accept rumors which the bearer will not confirm with a "Yes, you may quote me" guarantee of good faith.
5. You take the initiative in giving a fallen man a second chance at life.
6. You offer a listening ear and an understanding heart no matter what someone has been or done.
7. You give genuine forgiveness to those who betray you without waiting for their repayment or even their requests.

8. You offer self-forgetful love to all those about you.[1]

I do not believe any of us can do all of these things all of the time, but I do believe we can try. When I can't answer, "Yes, I am willing," I renew my commitment to those three steps to spiritual maturity: reading the Bible, praying for God's guidance and help, and being open to the Holy Spirit.

My friends and I have set an unwritten rule for our get-togethers: No gossip!—no matter how inquisitive we are about some new rumor. Instead we talk about the books we are reading and exchange a thought or passage of Scripture that has particularly encouraged us.

Unfortunately many friends have what might be called the Whistler-Wilde relationship. The essence of this friendship became obvious after a London newspaper printed the following bit of gossip. "James McNeill Whistler and Oscar Wilde were seen yesterday at Brighton, talking as usual about themselves."

The comment prompted Whistler to send a copy of the article to Wilde with a note: "I wish these reporters would be accurate: If you remember, Oscar, we were talking about me."

Wilde then responded with the following telegram: "It is true, Jimmie, we were talking about you, but I was thinking of myself!"

Obviously we must be listening to others, rather than thinking about ourselves, to have an encouragement ministry. Once I open my mind to others I have less time to worry about my own concerns and am better able to deal with them.

Jesus often put others' needs above his own. Just before the feeding of the five thousand, he suggested to the disciples, "Let's get away from the crowds for a while and rest" (Mark 6:31 TLB). So many people were coming and going that they had scarcely had time to eat.

But when the crowd saw Jesus and the disciples get into their boat and row to a quieter spot, many people ran ahead on the shore and met the boat when it landed. Jesus saw the people, and "had pity on them because they were like sheep without a shepherd" (v. 34 TLB).

Instead of retiring, he stayed with the crowd and taught them until dinner time. Then he told his disciples to feed the multitude (see v. 37).

The old Swedish proverb is true; "Shared joy is double joy; shared sorrow is half sorrow."

There are many different ways to encourage friends, neighbors, and coworkers. One of my age-conscious friends was having a birthday; but, for fear of revealing her age, she said she did not want a party of any kind. The night before her birthday, I went to her house and tied a giant bow of red ribbon around the tree outside her window so she would see it first thing in the morning. It marked the date just as joyously as a party.

When I bake, I make a double batch of cookies or rolls and put a dozen or so in a box for a gift. I always know someone who appreciates a few goodies. Or I call a neighbor who seems especially tired or busy and tell her not to cook supper. "I'd like to treat you and your family tonight." Just before dinner, I take a hot dish, some biscuits, and a freshly baked pie to her house. I often don't wait for an emergency to offer encouragement.

Once I wanted to encourage a friend whose father had died some weeks earlier, but I had no money to buy flowers. I filled a vase with long, dry spaghetti and fastened a shoestring bow around the noodles. The attached card read: "Hope you don't mind the noodles. I just wanted you to know we love you oodles!"

The next day I received a note in the mail: "Somehow I knew you wouldn't forget. I hope you don't mind; we ate the spaghett'!"

Sometimes when a friend is going through tough times, I send a verse that particularly applies to the situation each day for a week. Occasionally I have to revise my tactics, as I did after I suggested that a girl call me collect if she needed someone to talk to. The cost of the long distance calls led me to send her a box of stamps and some stationery, which served just as well and cost much less.

Once a month, my neighborhood friends and I get together for an encouragement party. We have dessert together as we brainstorm one-liners and verses for encouragement notes. Some are funny, some zany—even ridiculous—but all of them carry a message of care and love.

We openly discuss our experiences and feelings, which we have noted in a journal during the month. Talking about our problems helps us realize that we all face much the same difficulties. The grass is not greener on the other side of the fence;

it's as brown there at times as it is here.

We always share biblical insights that have helped us through our difficulties. Then together we pick one particular verse of Scripture to memorize during the next month.

Sometimes we read a Christian book during the month and discuss it at our next meeting. Long ago we pooled our resources to establish a private lending library to which each of us contributes a book a year. (Some of the books suggested at the end of each chapter are in our encouragement library.) All of us pray for encouragement for each other and for the discouraged persons we have added to our list.

My friend Shirley, who had worked efficiently in a local office for many years, shared her experience at one encouragement party. When the office manager suddenly quit, Shirley was so sure she would get the job that she began to plan, not only the changes she would make in the office routine, but a new wardrobe and a hairdo which would suit her new position.

Several days later, the executive manager called Shirley into his office. "You have been such a pillar around here, Shirley, that I have a special request of you," he said. Shirley felt certain his next words would be: "We have decided to make you the new office manager."

He began the way she had expected, "As you know, we need a new office manager....I feel you could be the person...to personally encourage and help the new fellow we have chosen for the job."

Shirley nodded, spoke some semblance of "Well,

I'll try to help," and left the office as soon as possible. In the next hour, she wrote several resignations, all listing very explicit reasons why she should leave immediately. In her hurt and disappointment, she prayed to the Lord for comfort and guidance: "Am I right to resign? Or is this where you want me to be?" She heard the Lord telling her to wait before making a definite decision.

Two days later, she was again called into the executive manager's office, this time to meet the new office manager, a tall, distinguished-looking man with dark curly hair, streaked with gray. His smile and ready greeting seemed to denote confidence and leadership.

"Shirley will be your right-hand woman for as long as you need her help," the boss said to Mike.

In the next few weeks Shirley's first assessment of Mike was verified: He quickly learned the office procedures and began to make some of the changes she had wanted to make. At the same time he freely acknowledged his appreciation to Shirley for her help and advice.

Eventually Shirley was able to tell Mike about her initial bitterness toward him and how she had been able to overcome it. After weeks and months of Shirley's enthusiastic encouragement, Mike accepted Jesus Christ as his personal Savior.

Shirley could have quit her job. She could have moved to another job where other unfair situations might have occurred. Instead the power of God's love in her life enabled her to overcome her bitterness and encourage another soul to Christ.

Each of us has the opportunity to serve the Lord

as Shirley did, for we touch the lives of our friends every day. I try to live out the truth in Proverbs 17: "A true friend is always loyal, and a brother is born to help in time of need" (v. 17 TLB).

Can you think of a friend who could use some encouragement today? A few seconds of your time might change a friend's life—and yours, too!

Thought you could use this little verse,
And what it has to say,
To add a little encouragement
And brighten up your day!

No lengthy words of advice,
None of that will do.
Just a verse to say that I care
And will be remembering you.

There is nothing like a friend,
Especially one like you,
One in whom I put my trust
Those are very few.

I see your home out my window.
I am pleased to know you're there.
It is great to have neighbors
For whom I really care.

There is a sense of belonging,
A feeling of pride,
Knowing we are living
Side by side.

The Friendship Factor by Alan L. McGinnis (Augsburg)

The Seasons of Friendship by Ruth Senter (Zondervan)

Friendship Evangelism by Arthur McPhee (Zondervan)

God Can Make It Happen by Johnston Rank (Victor)

Caring Enough To Forgive by David Augsburger (Regal)

Notes

Chapter 5

Encouraging
Your Parents

In October of 1982 I was asked to speak on encouragement to a women's group. Since my fond childhood memories were of loving parents, I decided to include a few ways to encourage parents. I was not prepared for the response that followed my talk.

Immediately after I concluded, a heavyset, poorly dressed woman walked up and said, with a cold and distant look in her eyes, "I would never do any of those things for my parents! The only thing I would deliver to their door is a bomb, which I hope would blow up and take them out of my life forever. They never cared about me. Why would I try to please them now?"

When I hesitated, she added, "Come on, sister, where's your answer for that one?"

I had none. The hate that radiated from this woman's eyes was so intense her words seared my heart. I watched her stomp toward the door, feeling I had failed her.

Next, a tiny, delicate girl inched her way to the front. "I'd like to be able to encourage my parents, but I can't," she admitted. "When I was a teenager, I became pregnant and my parents arranged for an abortion. Now I fight this memory every day of my life! I just can't forgive them for the pain they caused me!"

For the next several days, my mailbox was filled with letters from women who had been too embarrassed to come forward that night.

Pam had been an unplanned baby and had felt rejected and unwanted all her life. Her parents had openly accused her of being the source of their marital strife, which made her feel responsible for her mother's extreme unhappiness. Pam had begun to hate herself, and when she married, she had transferred her parents' rejection to her husband whom she felt did not love her. She could not even believe that God cared for her.

Terri had been physically, sexually, and verbally abused by her stepfather. Still struggling with the death of her own father, she became even more confused and bitter by the injustice of her stepfather's acts. After she married and became a mother, Terri was terrified that she would similarly mistreat her children. Anytime she became angry with them, she would feel depressed and guilty. Sometimes she even ran away from her family.

Each one of us experiences some hurts from parents who are tired, upset, or angry; but these women had felt hated and rejected. I wondered how many others suffered such trauma. It became obvious that some people could not minister to their parents until their own wounds had been healed.

I began to study books on inner healing and forgiveness, like *Set Free* by Betty Tapscott and *Free At Last* by Gloria Lundstrom, and to seek out Christians who had received healing from painful childhood memories. I searched for Scripture that dealt with healing and prayed for the women who had written to me. Then I began to answer these letters and to talk to some of the women personally.

I told Pam, who had always felt unwanted, that Jesus could heal her wounds and showed her the passage in 1 Peter 2: "For his wounds [on the cross] have healed ours!" (v. 24 TLB).

"If we do not accept his ability to heal us," I said, "we are rejecting him and the suffering he endured."

The thought of rejecting Jesus, particularly the Christ she could picture hanging on the cross, made Pam's eyes cloud with tears. Together we walked back through Pam's past and talked out each hurtful memory, claiming Psalm 147:3: The Lord "heals the broken-hearted, binding up their wounds" (TLB).

Pam's unplanned birth was not her fault. Instead of an awkward burden, she was God's special creation. God loved and accepted her just as she was, no matter what her background or family.

I suspected that Pam's deep emotional problems caused the migraine headaches she often experienced, so I told her of Cecil Osborne's observation in his book, *The Art of Understanding Yourself*: "A grudge creates stress, and continued stress is destructive. It paves the way for a host of physical symptoms: ulcers, heart attacks, asthma, migraine headaches, colitis, rheumatoid arthritis, and many others."[1]

That day Jesus walked with us through Pam's memory and began to heal her emotional and physical problems. In the next weeks, she began therapy with a Christian psychologist who helped her realize that she was never responsible for her parents' marital problems.

Soon she was able to accept her husband's love. Their fourteen-year-old marriage finally blossomed and grew as they studied God's Word together. They began monthly encouragement parties providing the opportunity for couples from their neighborhood and church to share their problems. Two very special guests were present at the last one I attended—Pam's parents. Once Pam was able to forgive her mother, she was also able to reach out to her in love.

Terri had spent a lot of money consulting psychologists and psychiatrists about her depression, which grew out of her stepfather's sexual abuse. She would be helped for a while after a session, but she would return a few weeks later more depressed than before. Because of her abused childhood, Terri was unable to give herself sexually to her husband. Finally he had become unfaithful. This caused Terri to feel like a complete failure, and she attempted suicide.

I knew that Terri needed to learn to give uncondi-
tional forgiveness to those who had hurt her, so I
shared my own struggles and the power God had
given me. I concluded by saying, "God has already
forgiven you and your stepfather, Terri. He tells us
in Hebrews 10: 'I will never again remember their
sins and lawless deeds' (v. 17 TLB).

"He's asking you to be as much like him as you
can, and in return he promises, 'For if you forgive
men their trespasses, your heavenly Father will
also forgive you' (Matt. 6:14 NKJV).

"At the same time he warns us all, 'But if you do
not forgive men their trespasses, neither will your
Father forgive your trespasses' " (v. 15 NKJV).

I asked her if we could pray together for her
healing, just as the disciples had done in Jesus'
days. "For the Lord promises in Matthew 18:18
that 'whatever you bind on earth will be bound in
heaven, and whatever you loose on earth will be
loosed in heaven' " (NKJV).

I took her hands in mine, and we sat together in
silence for a while. Then I prayed, "Satan, we are
not giving you the victory in Terri's life. A nega-
tive, unforgiving spirit comes only from you....Je-
sus, fill Terri with your positive love—powerful
above all else, able to conquer what seems to us im-
possible. Together Terri and I agree and ask it in
the name of Jesus. Amen."

In the days that followed Jesus filled Terri's life
with his love, joy, and peace. And after a year of
Bible study and prayer, Terri felt that she should
share her experiences with others. She was
amazed by how many other women lived under

the bondage of rage and guilt from the sexual abuse they had suffered in childhood.

She often mentions the most important gift God has given her—peace of mind. " 'For Christ himself is our way of peace,' " she testifies, quoting Ephesians 2:14. "He has made peace between us...by making us all one family, breaking down the wall of contempt that used to separate us' " (TLB).

Once Terri was able to unconditionally forgive her stepfather, she began to renew her acquaintance with her parents through letters. Surprised by a later phone call, he said little as Terri told him honestly of the bitterness she had felt against him and how her life had been affected by it.

Although he was unable to admit it, Terri sensed that guilt also clouded his life, so she continued to reach out to him and her mother with letters and phone calls. Finally they began to visit Terri and her husband, and through Terri's dynamic sharing of her Christian witness, they eventually gave their hearts to the Lord and were freed from years of pain and guilt.

Perhaps some of you who are reading this book need inner healing because of your memories of alcoholic or divorced parents; unwarranted, harsh criticism; undue comparison to your brother or sister; or physical and sexual abuse. Although some of these hurts are not as grave as others, all can cause problems in your life if you are not healed. And they will keep you from ministering to others as God wants you to. You might wish to walk with me through the following steps, which I always use when I minister to someone who needs inner healing:

1. Ask for and receive God's forgiveness.
2. Seek the root of your pain and let Jesus heal and cleanse it completely.
3. Bind Satan's negative forces and allow God to control and renew your thoughts.
4. Submit your whole life and mind to God's will, instead of your own selfish desires.

If you feel your sin is too great, remember some of God's people in the Bible. King David, one of the most effective kings of Israel, committed adultery with Bathsheba and then had her husband killed in battle. But David confessed his sins, asked for God's forgiveness, and received the gift of peace. He went on to unite the divided kingdom of Israel and change it from a weak country to a strong nation.

Saul of Tarsus participated in killing many Christians before he made his own commitment to the Lord. In Acts 7, we see him watching the stoning of Stephen, who cries out before he dies, "Lord, don't charge them with this sin!" (v. 60 TLB). When Jesus confronted Saul on the road to Damascus and Saul finally came to believe in him, Saul must have felt great shame and guilt. Yet God forgave him and gave Saul (who became the apostle Paul) the power to convert most of the Mediterranean world.

Once we have forgiven our parents for past

hurts, we are able to minister to them. Pat and Don, friends of ours from a neighboring town, both received healing from their memories. For years Pat had felt that her parents were disappointed in her because she had not been an ideal teenager. When she was still young, Pat left home to live "her own life" and had not contacted her parents since.

After Pat accepted Christ into her life, she wanted to contact her parents and restore a relationship with them. She began sending them notes, telling them where she was and what she was doing, about her husband, Don, and their small son. Sometimes when she didn't have any information to share or was unsure of what to say, she simply sent greeting cards signed with her name.

On Mother's Day, she sent a floral arrangement and a card that said, "I love you." On Father's Day, she wrote a long letter to her father, describing her salvation and healing and expressing her hope that he would someday find the same peace and joy. On the bottom of the last page, she wrote: "I love you."

Several weeks later, Pat's parents arrived at her home in tears. They had given their lives to Christ before receiving Pat's letter, and now they asked for Pat's forgiveness. That day they met their grandchild for the first time.

Pat's husband, Don, harbored a different childhood bitterness. His father, a vice-president of a large computer company, never seemed to have much time for Don, who idolized his dad. One of the few happy memories Don had of times they had shared together was one day when they had ridden horses, hired from a nearby stable, through the multicolored autumn woods.

Don's hobby was wood-carving. During the months he spent carving a statue of a horse for his dad, Don also prayed for his dad's salvation. Once the wooden horse was completed, Don decided to take it personally to his father at their family home, which was three hours away.

His mother greeted Don and his wife, Pat, and their four-year-old son, Todd, warmly, but his dad was out of town on business. Although Don still has not become really close to his father, he has forgiven his dad for the rejection he felt and has been able to be a loving father to his own son. He has never been too busy to go bike riding in the woods or to build model airplanes.

Send a note to your parents today to enrich an already good relationship—or to begin to melt the ice in a relationship that has grown cold. Reach out with the same forgiving love God has given you.

I love you, Mom,
For all you've done for me,
For all the loving sacrifice
That I'm just beginning to see.

There are words we never spoke,
Things we never shared,
But you were always there.
I always knew you cared!

Did you ever think that someday
You would get this note of love?
I simply wanted to tell you
How much you are really thought of.

As a parent you were wonderful.
But now I've come to know
In the last year, you have become my friend.
I really love you so.

Mom and Dad, I love you.
Although it's hard for me to say.
Christ is walking beside me and
I'm growing every day.

Love, Acceptance, and Forgiveness by Jerry Cook with Stanley C. Baldwin (Regal Books)

All Things Are Possible Thru Prayer by Charles L. Allen (Spire Books)

Tough Times Never Last, But Tough People Do by Robert Schuller (Thomas Nelson Publishers)

Set Free Through Healing of Memories by Betty Tapscott (Hunter Publishing)

Lonely, But Never Alone by Nicky Cruz (Zondervan)

Notes

Chapter 6

Encouraging
Our Senior
Saints

It was just "one of those days." I had baked a pot of beans and some rolls for Mrs. Henning, one of the two older people I visit each week in our local nursing home. She has her own little suite—a bedroom, a kitchen, and a small sitting room—and likes to entertain Landon and me for lunch every Tuesday. As I opened the door of our small car, Landon in one arm and our care package in the other, I didn't notice that his scarf was wrapped around the box. Too late! The care package flipped over and the pot of beans, which had bubbled all over my oven during the morning, tumbled onto the rug in the back seat.

In spite of the mishaps, I cleaned up the mess and we drove off. I still had fresh rolls and homemade jelly as a treat for Mrs. Henning, and I knew she would be happy to see me and my rosy-faced toddler son.

Encouraging ailing senior citizens like Mrs. Henning has not always been easy for me. I had always been healthy and could never understand why people sat and complained rather than "got up and got going." But after I suffered my own strange illness and had to depend on others for help, I developed a great deal of compassion for those who suffered from physical illness, whatever the cause.

As she had on past visits, Mrs. Henning held tightly to my arm for the entire visit while she recited Bible verses and remembrances from her past. Her possessive grip led me to believe that no one had visited her since my last trip.

At the end of my visit we walked arm-in-arm down the sterile, white-painted hall. I paused to say hello to Mrs. Nelson, who sat in the corner of the hallway, staring out the window with vacant eyes, her mind in neutral.

"I should've taken more time with my children," I heard her mumbling. "You know," she added, "maybe they would've been happier in life...Yes, yes, I failed as a mother." That thought must have haunted her every day.

When I got to the front door, the big leather armchair placed right near the entrance was empty. Mr. Patterson always sat in the chair so he could observe everyone who came in and out, though he pretended not to care. I always spoke to him, even though his usual reply was a "humph!"

The previous week, when I had been so busy

pulling Landon into his snowsuit that I had forgotten to say hi, Mr. Patterson had tapped his cane loudly on the floor to summon my attention.

Now I asked the nurse at the front desk, "Is Mr. Patterson sick?"

"No," she answered. "He'd been neglecting his meals for the past month; he seemed to just give up. He died a few days ago."

"What about Mrs. Nelson?" I asked anxiously. "She doesn't look well to me."

"She's OK. It's just that no one ever visits her. At least 450 of the 600 people in the home never receive visitors or word from outside. They withdraw into their own private world from sheer loneliness!"

Driving home that day, I kept remembering the nurse's statistics. How could so many people be left to live out their lives alone?

Most older people suffer from loneliness, the result of breaking their connections with family and friends and former occupations. Robert D. Lauder writes, "Loneliness is the feel of not really mattering to anyone." As people get older, they face the reality of rejection and the ensuing insecurity, so the best encouragement we can offer to senior saints is our fellowship.

Pete, the dear old man I also visit at the nursing home, comes to our house for dinner once a month. Our children are able to look past his hearing aid and walker and see someone who's lots of fun. When he is feeling well, Pete tells them stories. When he doesn't have strength for longer endeavors, he sits on the sofa surrounded by three curious boys and shows them how to make bird calls.

Once in a while, the kids send Pete homemade cards with their own verses of encouragement. Sometimes we smuggle a piece of cake from a special celebration into the nursing home; old age has not diminished Pete's sweet tooth. His eyesight is failing so we collect large print, easy-to-read materials for him to read with the aid of a magnifying glass. We also subscribe to two magazines for Pete: *Mature Living* (127 9th Avenue N., Nashville, TN 37234) and *Mature Years* (201 8th Avenue S., Nashville, TN 37202).

Pete fears the future even though he is a Christian. We never evade the subject of death when Pete mentions it. We remind him of his friend, Jesus, who will greet him in the next life, and has promised, "Most assuredly, I say to you, he who believes in Me has everlasting life" (John 6:47 NKJV) and "what we suffer now is nothing compared to the glory he will give us later" (Rom. 8:18 TLB).

We often share verses with Pete that tell him the Lord is with him each day, such as "Be strong! Be courageous! Do not be afraid...! For the Lord your God will be with you. He will neither fail you nor forsake you" (Deut. 31:6 TLB). Cutting the conversation short or refusing to discuss the topic of death with Pete would only increase his fear and frustration.

We had known Pete for some time before he asked us to do him a special favor: His feet hurt him so badly, he wanted someone to rub them. I got a basin, towel, and lotion, and the two oldest boys and I each took turns rubbing and powdering

Pete's feet. As he pulled the covers back over his gnarled, calloused feet, he said, "Thank you. That's just what Jesus would have done."

It has not been easy to give Pete's feet this treatment. His toes are crooked and sweaty, and often his feet smell like a gymnasium. He usually forgets that we have rubbed his feet or done other things for him, but that is not important to us since the Lord knows we are caring for him.

God calls us to encourage everyone, not just the lovely and lovable. And He often calls us to serve without recognition. At the same time that a friend is serving as president of the church women's group, you may be called by the Lord to read the Bible or an inspirational book to an elderly person in some out-of-the-way health-care facility.

Leonard Bernstein, the composer and retired conductor of the New York Philharmonic, once said that second fiddle was the most difficult instrument to play. "I get plenty of first violinists, but to find one who plays second violin with as much enthusiasm or second flute or horn, now that's a problem. And yet if no one plays second, we have no harmony."

Many of us are called to serve with the unselfish love Paul describes in Philippians 2: "Don't be selfish; don't live to make a good impression on others. Be humble, thinking of others as better than yourself. Don't just think about your own affairs, but be interested in others, too, and in what they are doing" (vv. 3-4 TLB).

Jane, a nurse's aide in a senior citizen apartment building, noticed that Pearl O'Conner, a bright, energetic widow in her seventies, had begun to slide slowly into depression. She was often absent from meals and group activities, spending all her time alone in her room without any interest in hobbies or outside involvement. Knowing that Pearl's only son and his family lived on the West Coast and were unable to visit more than a couple times a year, Jane decided to adopt Pearl. She began to visit her even though Pearl said she wished to be left alone. "The sooner I am in heaven, the better it will be for everyone," Pearl vowed.

Still Jane persisted; she listened to Pearl's remembrances of the "old days" and how she and her husband had endured the hardships of the Depression. Soon Pearl began to comb her hair and set the table in her room for tea on the days Jane visited. Next Jane encouraged Pearl to join some of the other women for their craft sessions and occasional tea parties. After some hesitation, Pearl ventured down and was soon chattering with them.

One day when Jane went to visit Pearl, a paper was taped to the door: "Sorry I missed you, Jane. I've gone shopping with a few friends. See you next time."

Jane smiled; her encouragement had helped a lonely, depressed woman learn to cope with her new life.

Widows like Pearl and Mrs. Henning and Mrs. Nelson, who felt she had failed her children, need to be reminded of the Lord's promise in Isaiah 54:

Do not fear,
    for you will not be ashamed;

Nor be disgraced,
   for you will not be put to shame;
For you will forget the shame of your youth,
And will not remember the reproach of
   your widowhood anymore,
For your Maker is your husband (vv. 4-5 NKJV).

Every time I begin to think an older person might not respond to encouragement because of weakness or sickness, I remember this story of John Quincy Adams's later years. One day John Adams was slowly and feebly walking down a street in Boston when an old friend stopped him to shake his trembling hand and ask, "And how is John Quincy Adams today?"

"Thank you," replied the ex-president, "John Quincy Adams is well, quite well, I thank you. But the house in which he lives at present is becoming quite dilapidated. It is tottering upon its foundation. Its roof is pretty well worn out. Its walls are much shattered, and it trembles with every wind. The old house is becoming almost uninhabitable, and I think John Quincy Adams will have to move out of it soon. But he himself is quite well, quite well."

Each old saint lives in a rather battered house, which has been blown and weathered by the winds of our imperfect world. But the spirit that is the essence of the person's being is still alive and well within that house and will respond to conversation and attention, even if that response is only a smile or a wrinkle at the corner of an eye.

In the same chapter of Isaiah, the Lord also promises his people:

For the mountains shall depart
And the hills be removed,
But My kindness shall not depart
    from you.
Nor shall My covenant of peace be removed (v. 10 NKJV).

The Lord keeps this promise through his people on earth, Christians who are called to " 'love each other just as much as I love you. Your strong love for each other will prove to the world that you are my disciples' " (John 13:34-35 TLB).

Is there a nursing home in your area? Ask the administration office for a list of older folks who do not receive visitors. Encourage the older saints in your own family and neighborhood. Reach out in love to these saints who will soon see the Lord.

Just wanted you to know
You are never alone.
God was thinking about you today and—
so was I.

Isn't God's love great!
He's all-powerful, in control of every situation.
He's always with us, awaiting our reach.
I lifted you up to Him today.
And He heard my prayer,

Just when you think you're all alone,
God taps softly on your memory,
And says,
"Lo, I am with you always" (Matt. 28:20 NKJV).

Have you some days when you're feeling down?
When life seems long and slow?
Try reading God's Word of victories ahead.
The glory of God will show.

Your life has changed all around you.
Things come and go through the years.
But God's still standing, planted firm,
Lasting through all the tears.

For all the time, love, and memories we've
shared.
I thank God every day for you.
For all the joy, peace, and victory I know,
I thank you every day for introducing me to God.

Verses To Encourage Anyone Who Is Ill or Suffering

"Give your burdens to the Lord. He will carry
them. He will not permit the godly to slip or fall"
(Ps. 55:22 TLB).

"Let him have all your worries and cares, for he is
always thinking about you and watching every-
thing that concerns you" (1 Pet. 5:7 TLB).

"The eternal God is your Refuge,
And underneath are the everlasting arms;
He thrusts out your enemies before you" (Deut.
33:27 TLB).

Ten Good Things I Know about Retirement by J. Winston Pearce (Broadman)

What's Coming Next? by Lowell Lundstrom (Lundstrom Ministries)

A Guide to Caring for and Coping with Aging Parents by John Gillies (Thomas Nelson)

If You're over the Hill, You Ought To Be Picking Up Speed by Carl Malz (Lundstrom Ministries)

The Tender Touch by Rexella Van Impe (Thomas Nelson Publishers)

God Calling (a devotional) by A.J. Russell (Spire Books)

Notes

Chapter 7

Encouraging
Your Pastor

The pastor knew it wouldn't be long before those in the congregation who were nodding sleepily would be jarred awake by the morning's message. He had prayed about this sermon for weeks, since he knew his remarks about fighting and factions within the church would offend some members. Would his people realize that the Lord was calling them to repent, or would they strike out at him for bringing up issues they wished to ignore?

All too often, a pastor who dares to take a stand, like the man I just described, later finds himself alone in his study, his head in his hands, his mind filled with the harsh words of those parishioners who were brazen enough to criticize him directly and with the insinuations and secondhand comments of those who weren't. No wonder some pastors give up in despair.

Church members today often expect their pastor

to fit perfectly the qualifications Paul suggested to Titus when he was looking for pastors for the cities of Crete:

> These pastors must be men of blameless lives because they are God's ministers. They must not be proud or impatient; they must not be drunkards or fighters or greedy for money. They must enjoy having guests in their homes and must love all that is good. They must be sensible men, and fair. They must be clean minded and level headed. Their belief in the truth which they have been taught must be strong and steadfast, so that they will be able to teach it to others and show those who disagree with them where they are wrong (Tit. 1:7-9 TLB).

Most ministers are all of these things—at some time. But no human being can be perfect all the time. If we think so, we are denying Adam's fall in the Garden of Eden. Our pastors try to be as nearly perfect as human beings can be, but their jobs are far from easy. Many pastors must be teachers, preachers, counselors, friends, and business managers—sounds very close to the proverbial "jack-of-all-trades."

They need help from members of their congregation. In fact, many Christians are beginning to stress the ministry of the laity, the responsibility of church members to assist in some of the work traditionally thought to be "the preacher's job": visiting the sick, counseling people within the church (often under the direction of the minister or a professional counselor), leading adult Bible study groups, and even performing services at convalescent homes.

All too often ministers are begging for parishioners to do even the jobs that have always been the responsibility of the laity. The following story may be nearer truth than myth. Every Monday morning a certain pastor was seen standing beside the railroad tracks, watching the trains whiz by. People in the town became worried that the pastor might be thinking of hurling himself in front of an oncoming train, so one gentleman finally asked him why he kept up this unusual practice.

"After all week at the church, I like to spend my day off watching the trains," the pastor replied. "They're the only thing in town that doesn't have to be pushed or pulled!"

Obviously, the board of deacons or elders or vestry has a particular responsibility to the pastor. The word which is translated *deacon* appears only a few times in Scripture and each time it means "servant." Deacons were first chosen as assistants to the disciples. The explosive growth of the early church made it impossible for the disciples to minister to all the people.

Deacons and board members who seek to know a pastor and understand his interpretation of doctrine and his style of ministry can communicate better with him and stand behind him if controversy arises. Board members and other members of the church can always pray for their minister.

In his book, *How to Support Your Pastor*, David Mains, host of the "Chapel of the Air," tells of the ministry he and his wife, Karen, found after he resigned his position as pastor of Circle Church in downtown Chicago. They became lay members of a church in Wheaton, Illinois.

The Mainses knew from firsthand experience that pastors are the targets of the enemy whenever a church manifests signs of real life. But few church members realize the forces of evil that are unleashed against their minister.

"Maybe we can bring the gift of intercessory prayer to this church," David suggested.

"Especially for the pastors," Karen added. And so their ministry began.

David Mains asks these rhetorical questions: "What would happen if, on the way to church in the car, families prayed together for pastors and teachers and musicians? Or what if some of us trained ourselves to get up early on Sunday morning, not to read the paper but to remind the Lord of his servant's needs? Or what if two or three or more Christians fasted on Saturday so that the presence of the Lord would be felt in power on Sunday?"[1]

An incident that happened to evangelist Dwight Moody in London is just one example of the power that would be unleashed:

> There was an invalid woman who had heard of Moody's work in America. She had been asking God to send him to London. Her sister was present at the church that Sunday morning and upon returning home asked, "Guess who preached to us today?"
>
> One pulpit supply after another was named but none was correct. "Ah, ha," the questioner said. "It was Mr. Moody from Chicago."
>
> Instantly the sick woman turned pale. "This is an answer to my prayer," she gasped. "But if I had known he was to be at our church, I should have eaten nothing this morning but waited on God. Leave me alone. Don't let

anyone come to see me. Do not send me anything to eat."
And all that afternoon this saint gave herself to interces-
sory prayer.

As Moody preached that night he became conscious
there was a different atmosphere in the church, for the
power of God seemed to fall upon him and his hearers. As
he drew to a close, he felt strongly led to give an invita-
tion, asking all who would like to accept Christ to rise.
Four or five hundred stood to their feet. Taken aback,
Moody thought they must have misunderstood, so he put
the question several ways. But, no, they had fully under-
stood. He then requested that these people go to an adjoin-
ing room, and quietly queried the pastor as to who they
all were.

"I don't know," said the minister.

"Are they your people?" probed Moody.

"Some of them."

"Are they Christians?"

"I don't think so."

In that adjoining room, Moody again strongly posed the
question of faith in Christ. There were still just as many
who rose. Confused, he instructed the inquirers to meet
with their pastor the following night. The next day he
left for Dublin, but as soon as he reached his destination
he received a telegram from the pastor stating he must re-
turn immediately, for a great revival had commenced.
There were more out the second night than the first!

This was the beginning of Moody's work as an interna-
tional evangelist. Out of these early efforts came the reli-
gious awakening of Great Britain and Ireland and the
salvation of thousands upon thousands of people through-
out the world.[2]

And all because one saint got down on her knees
and prayed. David Mains challenges all of us to join
her. "Revival won't just happen in this land with-
out thousands of preachers proclaiming God's
truth in power in a new way. And that won't occur

without countless people, such as yourself, turning from being passive critics and becoming active prayer supporters on behalf of God's chosen servants."[3]

He suggests that we ask ourselves some questions before we begin:

1. What are my pastor's responsibilities? One answer is to preach God's word. Then we would pray, "Lord, help _____ as he prepares his sermon this week. Help him to know which topics he should choose."
2. What pressures is my pastor facing? Much of intercessory prayer, Mains suggests, is just getting into the other person's shoes for a while.
3. What are my pastor's weaknesses?
4. What are his gifts? What dreams does he have?[4]

David Mains also suggests that we come right out and ask our ministers about their specific prayer needs.

Sometimes, when I know my pastor is discouraged, I invite him over for supper. A pastor once confided to me, "My people never invite me over. They all think I'm too busy or would rather not. I wish I could be the one to make that decision. Some nights I long for some friendly companionship. I want to be treated like a regular person."

Scripture is very specific about how we should treat our pastors. Let's begin with this verse from Luke 10: "the laborer is worthy of his wages" (v. 7 NKJV).

Is your pastor struggling financially? Are his family's needs being neglected because his congregation feels that a pastor should rely on the Lord for his income?

The official board of one church had called a meeting to raise funds for much-needed parsonage repairs. The house was literally falling apart and the pastor, knowing his family's hardship, made a stirring speech in the living room of their home.

Everyone was surprised when the most miserly member of the board rose and offered to start the fund with a contribution of five dollars. As he sat down a piece of plaster fell and hit him on the head. A trifle dazed, he rose again and said, "Reckon I'd better make that fifty dollars!"

A female voice from one corner of the room said: "Hit 'im again, Lord!"

When congregations are sensitive to the pastor's needs, the minister is free to think of more important things than his overdrafts.

A second verse we should all remember is Galatians 6:10: "Therefore, as we have opportunity, let us do good to all, especially to those who are of the household of faith" (NKJV).

Many people in the Bible cared for their leader's needs. The widow of Zarephath opened her home to the prophet Elijah—and also received God's blessings herself. Her bin of flour was never used up, her jar of oil never ran dry. And Elijah revived her son from a deadly illness (see 1 Kin. 17).

Mary and Martha, Lazarus's sisters, welcomed Jesus and his disciples to their home, and the Christians in Philippi sent Epaphroditus to minister to the apostle Paul when he was in prison in Rome.

Certainly the Lord expects us to extend the same love and encouragement to our leaders.

Every pastor needs to be appreciated. A small note of thanks, a word or gesture to acknowledge his hard work for the church, or a pat on the back as you leave the church and the words, "That was a great sermon!" encourage our pastors to continue the difficult work of caring for God's people. Some of us might even take a turn sitting in the front pews for a change. An intent look or a smile shows a pastor that you are interested and not just fulfilling an obligation.

Sometimes the pastor and his wife need an evening out. Offer your babysitting services or give them a gift certificate for a local restaurant. I occasionally double a favorite recipe and share it with my pastor's family. His wife may have spent all day on the phone, taking messages and counseling.

You might want to include her in your next shopping trip or send her a note of encouragement. She is a person, too, and carries a great responsibility. Ann Himmelberger Wald, a pastor's wife in Smithfield, Ohio, shared her search for friendship within her husband's church in *Partnership*, a magazine for wives in ministry.

"I *need* friends. Perhaps as a minister's wife, I feel this need even more strongly than other women. My husband works long hours. Many nights he is out late at meetings. Our extended families live more than a day's drive away. Friends fill a big gap in my life."[5]

Yet, Ann has had some frustrating experiences because of her position as the pastor's wife:

A friendship between a pastor's wife and a church member doesn't occur in a vacuum. It involves two people who care a lot about one church. What happens in the church can affect the friendship—whether it's a debate over the color of the sanctuary carpet or the merits of the King James translation over a modern one.

Because my husband represents the church, these debates tend to be subjective when they spill into my friendships. It's not just two friends differing. It's "Your husband is responsible for something I don't like." I can't escape the fact that my marriage colors my friendships and can even damage them.[6]

It's not easy for pastors' wives to find close friends who can share the frustrations of their ministry in the church. Often their friendships are dissolved by the situations that Ann Wald describes. But some of us may be able to support these women as friends by listening to their problems and refusing to take sides in church disputes. Other women may be able to reach out to them in areas of common interest: a shared hobby; children of the same age; the ups-and-downs of parenthood, or similar spiritual desires, such as a ministry of healing or prayer.

Pastors and their wives are finally beginning to admit their needs to their congregations, whereas they used to feel they had to look as if they "had it all together." Now that they have accepted the truth of their humanity, we need to reach out to them as we do to others. A sign on a church in Louisiana says: "In order to get to Heaven, take your flight training here!"

We are all copilots in this journey. We need to treat each other that way!

Alone in your study
With no one else there?
See Jesus in the stillness
And a room filled with our prayers.

It's not always easy.
I know your days are long.
But the music you help to render,
Is to an empty soul, a song.

I pray for you every day.
May God bring blessings to your family,
Just as you have brought blessings to ours.

This note is a thought of love
For the things you always share:
Your life, your time, your very self,
For the genuine way you care.

How to Support Your Pastor by David Mains (David C. Cook Publishing)

The Long Way Home by John P. Jewell, Jr. (Thomas Nelson Publishers)

Preacher: The Wit and Wisdom of Reverend Will B. Dunn by Doug Marlette (Thomas Nelson Publishers)

Chapter 8

Encouraging
People in
Your Church

After the Second World War, the townspeople of one devastated city in England were most concerned about the restoration of a large statue of Jesus Christ, which had been symbolic of Christ's help and guidance to generations before. It had stood in the old city square for many years, with hands outstretched in an attitude of invitation. The words carved on the pedestal read: "Come to me."

Master artists and sculptors worked for months reassembling the figure. But the fragments of the hands could not be found anywhere in the surrounding rubble. Finally someone suggested the artists fashion new hands.

Public outcry arose: "No! Leave him without hands!"

Today the restored statue of Christ stands in the square without his hands. The words carved on the new pedestal read: "Christ has no hands but ours."

The apostle Paul saw his life and the lives of other Christians as serving Christ in this way. He spent years writing letters to the churches he began throughout the Mediterranean world, helping these people to live and serve as a Christian community. In the Book of Romans he tells us that members of the church should work together just as well as parts of the human body: "Just as there are many parts to our bodies, so it is with Christ's body. We are all parts of it, and it takes every one of us to make it complete, for we each have different work to do. So we belong to each other, and each needs all the others" (Rom. 12:4-5 TLB).

Paul goes on to mention the types of service we each can perform:

> God has given each of us the ability to do certain things well. So if God has given you the ability to prophesy, then prophesy whenever you can—as often as your faith is strong enough to receive a message from God. If your gift is that of serving others, serve them well. If you are a teacher, do a good job of teaching....If God has given you money, be generous in helping others with it. If God has given you administrative ability and put you in charge of the work of others, take the responsibility seriously. Those who offer comfort to the sorrowing should do so with Christian cheer (vv. 6-8 TLB).

Sometimes Christians answer Paul's call in ways that are particularly unique to their own abilities. Vince Schell, a member of a small church in Boise,

Idaho, felt that God called him to be a "door-keeper." His story is just one example of Christian lay ministry. Each Sunday morning for the last twenty years, Vince has arrived at church at eight o'clock in the morning to do last minute cleaning chores. He shovels the snow in the winter; and in other seasons of the year, he washes the front windows so the sun will shine into the sanctuary.

About a half-hour before the service, Vince takes his position by the church door, ready to greet parishioners as they arrive.

"Good morning, Ross. Good morning, Luella. You're here early this morning. Oh, let me help you with that." Vince takes the posters Luella is carrying and helps her place them on the bulletin board.

Soon the bustle of others arriving fills the foyer. Opening the door, Vince greets each one with a loving handshake. Small boys, eager to shake hands just like their dads, extend their chubby little hands to Vince. Little girls skip up the sidewalk ahead of their parents, eager to be greeted. They wait shyly for the friendly hug Vince always gives them. Everyone feels the warmth of God's love as they enter his house of worship.

Vince's natural ability to remember names and faces so impressed one visitor that she later exclaimed in the adult class, "This is the first church I have attended where I have received such love and attention. Why, the man who greeted me at the door today remembered my name, and this is only the second time I've come. I'm going to come back again! I feel welcomed and accepted."

Vince's wife, Dorothy, says that Vince himself has benefited from his ministry. "As the years have passed, Vince's love for the church has grown even stronger. He has been blessed by members in the church thanking him for his work, but his desire to serve the Lord brings an inner peace that goes beyond the praise of others. The knowledge that he is doing God's will is enough reward."

Vince Schell reaches out to others from his genuine love of God and his desire to have others feel that love. The apostle Paul makes it very clear to the Romans—and to us!—that the Christian's commitment to serve others must be real. There is no room for hypocrisy:

> Don't just pretend that you love others: really love them....Love each other with brotherly affection and take delight in honoring each other....When God's children are in need, you be the one to help them out. And get into the habit of inviting guests home for dinner or, if they need lodging, for the night. When others are happy, be happy with them. If they are sad, share their sorrow. Work happily together. Don't try to act big. Don't try to get into the good graces of important people, but enjoy the company of ordinary folks (Rom. 12:9-16 TLB).

Certainly Paul is giving us our marching orders. He has painted a very accurate picture of Christians' ministry to one another in the church congregation. It's much deeper than the casual greeting on a Sunday morning, "Hi! How are you?" It's crying with someone when they are sad and laughing with them when they are glad.

Paul is asking us to do what one little girl did naturally when her playmate died: She immediately went over to visit the child's mother.

"Why did you go over there?" her father questioned when she returned, fearing that the child had just added to the confusion.

The little girl answered, "To comfort her mother."

"What could you do to comfort her?" her father asked increduously.

"I climbed up into her lap and cried with her!"

This is the fellowship Paul is suggesting. And more and more churches today are accepting Paul's challenge. Sometimes large churches, like the Crystal Cathedral in Los Angeles or Truro Episcopal Church in Virginia, organize into small discipleship or shepherding groups of ten or fifteen members, who meet together regularly to read the Bible and share their problems.

John Howe, rector of Truro Church, tells why the shepherding groups were begun: "We started with this concept: that there is no way you can belong to a parish of two thousand or twenty-five hundred members. You belong to maybe a dozen. There you get to know people, deeply, and they know you. There you really get to share each other's burdens. There your defenses can begin to come down, your masks come off, you get exposed as who and what you are—that's where you *belong.*"

God has given each of us different abilities and talents. What is yours? God may be calling you to serve as a Sunday school teacher, a member of the church board, or a member of the next bazaar committee. And he may be calling you to be an encourager in any one of these activities.

Paul reminds us that the members of the church are meant to be as dependent upon one another as the parts of the body are upon each other.

> God has made...many parts for our bodies and has put each part just where he wants it. What a strange thing a body would be if it had only one part! So he has made many parts, but still there is only one body.
>
> The eye can never say to the hand, "I don't need you." The head can't say to the feet, "I don't need you."
>
> And some of the parts that seem weakest and least important are really the most necessary. Yes, we are especially glad to have some parts that seem rather odd! And we carefully protect from the eyes of others those parts that should not be seen, while of course the parts that may be seen do not require this special care. So God has put the body together in such a way that extra honor and care are given to those parts that might otherwise seem less important. This makes for happiness among the parts, so that the parts have the same care for each other that they do for themselves. If one part suffers, all parts suffer with it, and if one part is honored, all the parts are glad.
>
> Now here is what I am trying to say: All of you together are the one body of Christ and each one of you is a separate and necessary part of it (1 Cor. 12:18-27 TLB).

Without doubt, God is calling us to encourage one another within the church family. But it is not easy to abandon our selfish desires to help another person. First, we must be plugged into the greatest power source of all time: the Holy Spirit.

God gives his spirit to Christians—both now and throughout the ages—so that we might accomplish the impossible! When the small group of Jews returned to Jerusalem after their seventy-year exile in Babylon and attempted to rebuild the temple, the work was halted by the king of Babylon. The task seemed impossible! Twenty years later, God told the prophet Zechariah to rebuild the temple: "Not by might, nor by power, but by my Spirit, says the Lord of Hosts—you will succeed because of my Spirit, though you are few and weak" (Zech. 4:6 TLB). Four years after the prophecy, the temple was completed.

Imagine a magnificent mansion sitting high on a lush, green hill, a brick walk leading up to the huge, mirrored door. Inside, crystal chandeliers hang from gold casings and magnificent candelabra adorn the walls. But the mansion is located in a remote area, which is not yet connected to electrical cables. Despite all the grandeur, there is no life. No power! The mansion is dark and dead. We are just as ineffective when we aren't filled by God's spirit.

Once the power is connected, we are able to reach out to others in genuine love, not only to church members but to others who come to the church for help, like the mother of three children who sits in the back pew and seems afraid to look others in the eye. She is abused by her husband, and is fearful for her children's future.

The Holy Spirit will enable us to: (1) see someone who is in need; (2) remember our past weaknesses and failures; and (3) show us how to deal with each individual situation.

Christians who are led by the Holy Spirit do not minister alone; they are covered by the grace and power of God. A friend once told me the story of a young mother who took her son to a performance of the famous pianist Paderewski to encourage her son's interest in the piano. They took their seats near the front of the concert hall, close to the majestic grand piano on the stage. As the mother was talking to a friend who happened to be sitting in the row behind them, the boy slipped away.

At eight o'clock, when the spotlights came on, and the audience quieted, the hall was filled with the sound of a small boy picking out the tune of "Twinkle, Twinkle Little Star" on the grand piano. Before his mother could retrieve her son, Paderewski appeared on stage and quickly moved to the keyboard.

He whispered to the boy, "Don't quit; keep playing." Paderewski reached down with his left hand and began filling in the bass part. Soon his right arm reached around the other side, encircling the child, to add a running obligato. Together the old master and the young child held the crowd mesmerized.

Unpolished as our own efforts may be, our Master surrounds us and whispers in our ear, "Don't quit. Keep playing."

I will never forget the day I called a girl whom I had felt led to pray for. I could not see the bottle of tranquilizers in her hand or know that she had finally decided to kill herself.

"I was so alone," she sobbed, "so discouraged. I didn't think God was listening. How did you know?" she asked me.

"I didn't," I admitted. But God did.

Some people in my church wondered why I was

drawn to this girl. We didn't seem to have much in common, since she was single and I was married. She wore too much make-up and flimsy blouses with rather low necklines. Still I knew the Lord was telling me to call her.

Jesus went out of his way to associate with those who really needed him, some of whom weren't known for their virtue—tax collectors like the apostle Matthew who cheated the people and was not much better than a thief. The Pharisees asked his disciples, " 'Why does your teacher associate with men like that?' " (Matt. 9:11 TLB).

Jesus replied, "Because people who are well don't need a doctor! It's the sick people who do!" Then he added, "It isn't your sacrifices and your gifts I want—I want you to be merciful" (v. 12 TLB).

Unfortunately, some Christians' commitment is closer to this description:

> I would like to buy $3.00 worth of God, please. Not enough to explode my soul or disturb my sleep, but just enough to equal a cup of warm milk, or a snooze in the sunshine. I don't want enough of Him to make me love a black man or pick beets with a migrant. I want ecstasy, not transformation; I want the warmth of the womb, not a new birth. I want a pound of the eternal in a paper sack. I would like $3.00 worth of God, please.[1]

With this kind of commitment, we are of no service whatsoever. Our churches do not grow. Our faith does not grow either.

Unfortunately Christians sometimes destroy the power of their witness by the backbiting, jealousy, and competition that exist within the church itself.

Paul told the Romans that "we...are one body in Christ" (Rom. 12:5 NKJV). Instead, we sometimes seem to be exploding like fireworks into small pieces and factions.

I have been told that wild donkeys of the great Northwest circle in, put their heads together, and kick outward when they are attacked by wolves—until the beasts are driven off or kicked to death!

Sometimes church members seem to do just the opposite. When the wolves attack, we put our tails together and kick one another to death!

Lowell Lundstrom once said, "I fear the church is the only species that kill their wounded."

But God has called us to another way. If you reach out to people who are facing the same discouragements, the same problems you are, you become an encourager. And sometimes, that's catching. The disease might infect your whole church!

Jonathan was such an encourager. He went to David when he learned that King Saul, Jonathan's own father, had ordered his soldiers to find David and kill him. At a moment when David was at his lowest, Jonathan was there to encourage him.

Jonathan was effective because he dispelled David's fear. He reminded David of God's promise to him: "You shall be king over Israel, and I shall be next to you. Even my father Saul knows that" (1 Sam. 23:17 NKJV).

Most people who are discouraged feel just as David did: They are afraid of the future or afraid of rejection or failure. Reminding others of the promises in God's Word is the first step to encouragement.

Jonathan also gave David confidence. "Do not fear, for the hand of Saul my father shall not find you" (v. 17 NKJV). Every discouraged person needs to be reminded that what they fear will probably not happen. Psychologists say that 95 percent of the things we fear never happen. After all, God has promised to bless and protect us.

Jonathan also gave David a promise for the future. Although David didn't know it, he was in God's "training program," being prepared to lead Israel into glory. All of us sometimes find our training program here on earth too difficult; then a friend needs to help us look ahead to see God's master plan for our lives.

Finally, Jonathan promised David companionship. "I shall be next to you," he said. Jonathan was willing to risk his own life and the anger of his father and king to stand by his friend. He knew that encouragement means more than a pat on the back!

Begin your own ministry of encouragement today. Someone you know is waiting and needs a moment of your time. You might be the person God has chosen to save someone from a deep depression or a godless life.

Is there a family who is suffering because the father is out of work? A small anonymous financial gift can encourage that family when they need it most. Perhaps you could open your home for a prayer and/or Bible study group. Sometimes people who have problems are more able to discuss them in a home atmosphere than in the church office.

Take a good look at the people in your church

next Sunday. Then use the note pages at the back of this book to list the names of those who need immediate encouragement.

I recently saw a Dennis the Menace cartoon, which portrayed encouragement very simply and profoundly.

Dennis and his friend were walking down the sidewalk on New Year's Day, listening to those around them wish each other a Happy New Year. "Do you think they really mean it?" Dennis asked his friend.

"Naw, they say it 'cause it's polite," the realistic friend replied.

Just then Mrs. Wilson called to the boys. "Happy New Year, boys. Come on in and have some apple pie!"

As Dennis and his friend gratefully devoured the hot apple pie, Dennis exclaimed, "Mrs. Wilson not only says, 'Happy New Year,' she *makes* it happen!"[2]

Our Father calls us to "make it happen." And he's calling you to begin right now!

During this time of sorrow
Our love and compassion we send.
For death is but life—winning is loss—
A beginning and not an end.

Thanks for your words of kindness.
You really made my day.
You were there when I needed someone
To encourage me on my way.

When we ask, "When?"
He answers, "In time."
When we ask, "Why?"
He assures, "You are Mine."

God knows your situation,
And only asks, "Let Me lead."
So trust and follow His wisdom.
He understands your need.

Faith Founded on Fact by John Warwick Montgomery (Thomas Nelson)

The Keeping Power of God by Herbert Lockyer (Thomas Nelson)

How You Can Pray with Power and Get Results by Lowell Lundstrom (Lundstrom Ministries)

How on Earth Can I Be Spiritual? by C. Sumner Wemp (Thomas Nelson)

Notes

Record Page

Name	Call	Visit	Letter	Date

Chapter Three

1. David Augsburger, *Be All You Can Be* (Carol Stream, IL.: Creation House, 1970), p.82.

2. George Sweeting, *Catch the Spirit of Love* (Wheaton, IL.: Victor Books, 1983), p.19.

3. Rudolf Dreikurs, M.D., with Vicky Soltz, R.N., *Children: The Challenge* (New York: Elsevier-Dutton, 1964), p.36.

Chapter Four

1. David Augsburger, *Be All You Can Be* (Carol Stream, IL.: Creation House), p.25.

Chapter Five

1. Cecil Osborne, *The Art of Understanding Yourself* (Grand Rapids: Zondervan, 1976), p.60.

Chapter Seven

1. David Mains, *How to Support Your Pastor* (Elgin, IL.: David C. Cook, 1980), p.10.

2. *Ibid.*, pp.22-23.

3. *Ibid.*, p.13.

4. *Ibid.*, pp.18-19.

5. Ann Himmelberger Wald, "Prescription for Healthy Friendships" *Partnership*, (March 1984): p.35.

6. *Ibid.*

Chapter Eight

1. Charles Swindoll, *Improving Your Serve* (Waco, TX.: Word Books, 1979), p.29.

2. Dennis the Menace cartoon, *Fathergram* (May 1983).

Notes

Notes